HAPPINESS IS A HABIT

GORDON POWELL

HAPPINESS

IS A

HABIT

CASTLE BOOKS

NEW YORK

DEDICATED

TO

MY CONGREGATION

ACKNOWLEDGMENTS

The author acknowledges his indebtedness to the following authors and is grateful for permission to quote from their work: Virginia Douglas Dawson and Betty Douglas Wilson, Dr. Leslie Weatherhead, Dr. Norman Vincent Peale, Dr. Dale Carnegie, Dr. A. Wylie Blue.

CONTENTS

INTRODUCTION

WHETHER the method for achieving happiness described in this book is original or not I do not know. What I do know is that, when sincerely and consistently practiced, it works.

One man put on fourteen pounds in weight within a few months of applying this system. Lest that should discourage reducers let me hasten to record the effects on a woman whose nerves had driven her on several occasions to seek treatment in a mental hospital. She improved so much that no further medical attention was necessary and today, without having added any excess weight, she looks ten years younger!

A business man at the age of fifty-four suffered

such a complete breakdown that his family feared he would never work again. Reading a newspaper article describing the effects of our system he decided to try it. Now he is one of the most robust people one could wish to meet, having completely regained his health of mind and body.

Already this introduction may sound like an advertisement for a new patent medicine. We are not, of course, advocating anything out of a bottle or in the shape of a pill. At the same time we are describing a "tonic."

In these days of psychosomatic medicine doctors are realizing more and more that sickness in the mind produces sickness in the body and, conversely, health in the mind produces health in the body. One medical authority goes so far as to claim that more than half the patients in hospital are there because of sickness which began in the mind or which has been aggravated by mental unhappiness.

Our "tonic" works at the mental and spiritual levels and we have tried it out on the largest mid-week congregation meeting in any church in the Southern Hemisphere, possibly in the world. In St. Stephen's Presbyterian Church opposite Parliament House in Sydney, Australia, over 1,000 people gather every Wednesday for a brief lunch hour service. The congregation is made up mostly of young men and women from neighboring offices, but it also includes parliamentarians from across the road, doctors, lawyers, bankers and other businessmen. Increasing numbers of patients are sent to the church by doctors and psychiatrists. The services are broadcast to thousands more both in New South Wales and in Queensland.

"Most people are about as happy as they make up their minds to be," said Abraham Lincoln. Apparently he did not make up his mind about it since there are few faces sadder than that of the great American president. Possibly he did make up his mind, but a most difficult wife and the cares of State made him forget. Elbert Hubbard put his finger on the trouble when he said, "Happiness is a habit, cultivate it."

How can you cultivate the habit of happiness? Pondering that question I was led to believe that the answer might be found in the "tonic prayer cards" we had instituted in the Collins Street Independent Church, Melbourne, Australia, and continued in a different form at St. Stephen's. Within the first year in Sydney we had printed over 130,000 of these cards, distributing them mainly to the 2,500 people who came to the three services a week. The cards were used at the Sunday services as well as on Wednesdays.

On the back of every card are printed these words, "What is in the conscious mind sinks down into the unconscious to influence our moods and our health. If we indulge in negative, resentful, unkind or impure thinking we become tense, unhappy, depressed, fear-ridden individuals. If we fill our minds with what is positive, worthy and beautiful, we gradually build integrated, poised, power-filled lives. Health and happiness depend on positive thinking and faith."

The front of the card is changed week by week, but always there is some great affirmation from Scripture. Some affirmations which have proved most helpful have been, "I will fear no evil: for Thou art with me," "This is the day which the Lord hath made; we will rejoice and be glad in it," "The Lord is my helper" and "Rejoice in the Lord."

The user of the card is urged to place it in a prominent position so that he will see it many times a day. Each time he catches sight of it he is reminded to repeat the great positive thought printed on it and this helps to drive out the negative thoughts which cause tension and depression.

In due course I came to apply this technique directly to the problem of happiness and plan a series of addresses on the principles of happiness as taught by Jesus Christ. Like many others I had assumed that the only happiness which concerned Him was the bliss of heaven or a happiness so highly spiritual that only great saints could attain to it. On checking

a concordance one day I was surprised to find that
the word "happiness" does not appear in the Authorized Version of the Bible at all. Seeking an explanation I found that the older and, perhaps, richer
word "blessedness" is used. Only then did I realize
that Jesus had much to say about the day to day
happiness of ordinary people like ourselves. Furthermore I realized that no lasting happiness could
be ours until we took to heart and made a perma-
nent feature of our lives the principles He laid down
on this subject.

Accordingly I selected twelve of His principles of
happiness and made them the basis of our tonic
cards and my weekly addresses for the next three
months. The addresses are reproduced here almost
as they were given together with the wording of the
tonic card at the end of each. The reader might care
to make a small card reproducing such texts or
prayers as he finds most helpful himself and keep it
handy in the office, the factory, the home or even
on the dashboard of his car.

At the beginning of the series a printed syllabus
was issued and members of the congregation, both
those in the church and those listening in, were invited to send to me descriptions of personal experiences to illustrate the effectiveness of the teachings
of Christ in regard to happiness. Many responded
as the following chapters will show. I am deeply

grateful to all who helped in this and in other ways. Most of all I must express my gratitude to my wife who has typed the manuscript and by her own constant happiness is the best proof I know that the principles laid down in the Sermon on the Mount still work today.

HAPPINESS IS A HABIT

CHAPTER ONE

SECRET GIVING

LLOYD DOUGLAS, who will go down in history as one of the greatest story-tellers of the twentieth century, was nearly fifty before he wrote his first novel.

In 1927 he was still settling in as the new minister of a large Congregational Church in Los Angeles. That winter he announced a series of three sermons on the general subject of "The Secrets of Exultant Living." In these sermons he tried to show people that religion could be a real power in their lives if they would only apply the simple principles of Jesus in an honest and practical way. For example, he referred them to the words of our Lord, "Take heed that ye do not your alms before men, to be seen of them." He told his Los Angeles congregation that if they heeded that advice and practiced it they would store up power in their personalities. So he preached that day on the power of secret giving known only to one's God. He pointed out that a magnificent relationship was there only waiting to be recognized. "Behold" said the Master, "I stand at the door and knock. If any man hear my voice and open the door, I will come in to him."

Lloyd Douglas preached three Sundays on this theme. The congregations increased and on the third Sunday a huge crowd gathered. Everybody seemed to be straining forward as though they were hearing some wonderful secret of living and were afraid of missing a single word. That day lunch was late because so many people stayed behind to tell the Minister that the sermon had helped them. Lloyd Douglas came home tired, but exhilarated. As the family sat down to their cold ham his wife said to him, "I was helped by your sermon today, Lloyd. I think for the first time I understand exactly what was meant by the idea of secret altruism." The two daughters both murmured something about the sermon inspiring them too, a most unusual happening. As Lloyd Douglas began to carve he said, "The idea has been there in the Bible for a long time, but its simplicity disguises its power. Once you try it you realize that you have laid hold of something. I wish I could get the meaning across to more people. If I have a message it is probably that."

"Why don't you put it into your novel?" said his daughter Betty as she buttered a piece of bread. Her father seemed transfixed with the carving knife and fork in his hands. Seconds passed and the other three looked at him. Then Mrs. Douglas said excitedly, "Is that it, Lloyd?" It was. Lloyd Douglas nodded, but remained silent. The family got the impression he was offering a prayer of thankfulness. So the novel, *Magnificent Obsession,* was born, based on the text, "Let not thy left hand know what thy right hand doeth." It went through more than fifty editions and for fourteen years was among the best-selling books in America. It led to Lloyd Douglas giving up the ministry and devoting his whole time to the writing of novels with a Christian message. His greatest achievement was *The Robe.*

It was said of that first novel, *Magnificent Obsession,* that the people who read it were never quite the same again. I believe that to be true. It is the story of a young ne'er-do-well, Bobby Merrick, playboy grandson of a millionaire, whose life was saved when the boom of his yacht knocked him unconscious and he fell into a lake. Fortunately for him an oxygen inhalator was available, but by a tragic coincidence at the very moment when his life was being saved because of it, the owner, Dr. Wayne

Hudson, suffering from a heart attack was breathing his last for want of the same machine. Recovering in Dr. Hudson's hospital, Bobby Merrick learned the truth and resolved to make amends by devoting his life to the same ideals as Dr. Hudson and, if possible, take his place as the most brilliant brain surgeon in the country. One day Bobby's friend, Tom Masterson, went to see the bereaved Mrs. Hudson who only recently had been married to the much-lamented doctor. She told him how all sorts of people had come wanting to give her money. They said they had been helped by Dr. Hudson, but he had always refused to take anything in return. Five different persons told her that he had said the same thing to them, "I have used it all up myself." They were mystified and wanted to know what it meant. At this stage nobody could supply the answer.

Meanwhile Bobby Merrick, pursuing his medical course, had discovered Dr. Hudson's secret journal, written in code. After long study he cracked the code and solved the mystery. Dr. Hudson, the materialistic doctor, had acquired a new philosophy of life from a monumental mason named Randolph. He saw that to release and enlarge personality it was necessary to build it into other personalities. To quarrel with a friend was to lose part of your own personality. To do good to others, without the world knowing about it and without receiving a worldly reward for doing it, was to enlarge your personality into the lives of others. At first Dr. Hudson didn't believe it, but he began to practice it in his own life and he found that it worked. His talents and powers were released. His ability to serve mankind through his skill as a brain surgeon was immeasurably enlarged. His personality really began to express itself.

Young Bobby Merrick, reading this journal, at first thought his great hero, Dr. Hudson, was mentally afflicted, but then one day, almost by accident, he applied the same principle to a poverty-stricken fellow student and he, too, found that it worked. As with Dr. Hudson, it became with him a Magnificent Obsession.

That in brief is the story which Lloyd Douglas told to express the truth which he had discovered in his own ministry. I can testify that from my own experience the same thing is true. I know several persons who do good to others and do it secretly in this sense, that nobody knows about it except myself because I transmit their gifts. Those who receive the gifts are happy, but their happiness is nothing compared with the happiness of those who give secretly. As Jesus said, "It is more blessed—it is a much happier thing—to give than to receive. Let not your left hand know what your right hand doeth." If you have never done it, I urge you to experiment with little acts of secret giving. I am sure you will find an increase of spiritual power and a deep sense of happiness.

For obvious reasons it would be impossible to give publicly an exact illustration of the principle, but here is a story to drive home the essential truth and it is something I can vouch for personally. My story begins on the 17th of June, 1907. On that day my greatly-honored predecessor, the Rev. John Ferguson, was concerned about one of his Sunday School teachers. Mrs. Parkhurst had recently been bereaved of her husband. She was in dire financial straits and had two boys to maintain, Donald, 10, and Frank, 13. The Rev. John Ferguson pondered the matter, no doubt he prayed about it, and then he wrote this letter:

Dear Mrs. Parkhurst,

I wish you to accept the enclosed from the Church Fund for assisting members in distress. Should you in after years be in a position to put the same back into the fund—why then it will go to assisting someone else in his or her distress. Meantime it is yours to enable you to go about and establish a business connection and get what you absolutely need. Wishing you brighter days and with a blessing for the boys.

Ever your pastor,
John Ferguson

The amount enclosed would not go very far today,

but in those days it was worth much to this distracted widow. It gave her new courage. It enabled her to get on her feet financially and to start life afresh. In due course the family moved to California where they prospered. In 1952 I received a letter from F. W. Parkhurst, contracting electrical engineer of Oakland, California, enclosing the Rev. John Ferguson's letter which he had just discovered among his mother's effects and saying that he did not know if this debt was ever repaid, but whether it was or not he would like us to accept the twenty-five dollars he enclosed as a donation to the Church Poor Fund.

For some time we had been seeking to raise enough dollars to buy copies of Sallman's picture of the head of Christ which were obtainable in the United States. I wrote to Mr. Parkhurst for permission to put the equivalent number of Australian pounds into the Poor Fund and use the dollars to buy the pictures. Most generously he insisted on sending out 1,500 copies and these were used to illustrate the syllabus of tonic cards based on the principles of happiness. This challenging and beautiful picture inspired and comforted many hundreds who received the syllabus. Since then, Frank Parkhurst, out of his present prosperity, has helped the Church in other ways. He assures me that it gives him immense pleasure to do so and I believe this is literally true.

What happiness must have come to the Rev. John Ferguson as he thought of that widow and her two boys making good, thanks, in part, to the encouragement and help he was able to give at a critical time! It is indeed more blessed to give than to receive and if we can give secretly or, as Jesus said, without our left hand knowing what our right hand doeth, it is a sure way of building up inward strength and happiness.

People seem to have the impression that Jesus was not concerned with happiness, or, if He was, it was only the happiness of heaven. That is nonsense. He may not have used the word "happiness" but He made many references to "blessings" and those who are "blessed." For instance the very first thing He said in the Sermon on the Mount was "Blessed are the poor in spirit, blessed are they that mourn, blessed are the meek, blessed are they that hunger and thirst after righteousness." Jesus came to make people happy and to make them happy in this world as well as the next.

He did that for two people I know, a Sydney business man and his wife. Although the husband had a good position and their home was a pleasant one with many comforts and indeed luxuries, a dark cloud of unhappiness had settled down over them and their nerves were going to pieces. They were not Church people. For years the only time they ever saw the inside of a Church was at a wedding or a funeral. One day the same newspaper article referred to earlier led the woman to listen-in to a service next day. The following Sunday she and her husband came to Church to worship God.

Meanwhile that outstanding Australian religious leader, the Rev. Alan Walker, was conducting his highly-successful "Mission to the Nation." It was reported that in six months a quarter of a million people attended the meetings addressed by Mr. Walker and it is believed that a million listeners heard the weekly mission broadcast. My business man and his wife were deeply impressed by the sincerity and sound common sense of Alan Walker and it challenged them to come forward to join the full membership of the Church. Writing to me at the time this man said:

"In the uncertainties of modern living, many have lost the capacity to think in any other terms than their own desires, pleasures, worries and troubles with the consequence of discontent and nerves so evident today. We are indeed grateful for the discovery of the way to a more peaceful, purposeful and less selfish outlook by the realization of the benefits of worship and the tolerance and charity which can only come from the words and teachings of God."

Does this not sum up the situation? In this modern world you have, on the one hand, people who leave

God out, live selfish and worldly lives and, sooner or later, pay the penalty in discontent, nerves and unhappiness. On the other hand those who discover God integrate their personalities and find a way of life which leads to harmony and happiness. As Professor William James expressed it after examining hundreds of such people, "They feel free, right and happy." This happiness is not the effervescent gaiety stimulated by alcohol or the artificial pleasures of this world, but the abiding contentment which comes from living in harmony with the rules of life laid down by the God Who created us all. These rules of life are the principles of happiness taught by Jesus Christ and are the subject of this book. They are principles which become second nature to those who believe in Christ and love Him. Through faith and love His spirit enters the soul and we experience the glorious liberty of the children of God.

TONIC CARD

LET NOT THY LEFT HAND KNOW
WHAT THY RIGHT HAND DOETH.
Matthew vi. 3.

What I spent I had,
What I kept I lost,
What I gave I have.

CHAPTER TWO

BIG-MINDEDNESS

THE SECOND PRINCIPLE of happiness I call, "Big-mindedness." It is summed up in our Lord's words in Matthew v. 7. "Blessed are the merciful, for they shall obtain mercy." In this case I prefer the translation by J. B. Phillips. Three hundred years ago the word "mercy" had a rich, warm meaning, much wider than its present narrow use in regard to the remission of punishment. I believe Phillips recaptures the power of our Lord's message by translating His words, "Happy are the kind-hearted, for they will have kindness shown to them."

If we are kind-hearted only because we want kindness shown to us that is a form of selfishness and

Christ's law of happiness will not work. That is not being big-minded. It is being little-minded. We all know the type of parent who makes himself or herself miserable because "the children are so ungrateful." Love doesn't do things in the expectation of reward. What we need to do is to cultivate the attitude of love and kindliness towards others, the attitude of big-mindedness regardless of reward. To do that let us remember three principles of Christ in the Sermon on the Mount summed up in the words "Blessed are the merciful."

I

The first principle is "Judge not that ye be not judged" (Matthew vii. 1). Once again I prefer Phillips' translation. In the original Greek the word "krino" is used, the word from which we get our word "criticize." Jesus surely did not forbid us to judge another person in the sense of judging him to be noble, good, generous, loving or virtuous in any other way. The context proves that He meant we were not to criticize others, not to find fault in others. We all have a tendency to do that, don't we? It boosts our ego to find the defects in others, but nobody ever got rid of his own faults by pointing out the faults of his neighbors. As one wise man said, "Hunt for the good points in the other fellow; he has to do the same with you."

Judge not, that ye be not judged. Do not criticize and you will not be criticized. My old friend, the world-famous evangelist, Dr. Lionel B. Fletcher, just before his death, sent me an excellent illustration of this principle from his own experience. Fifty years ago he went to his first church in the country. The most powerful man in the church was a black-bearded, black-eyed deacon who gave the young minister a feeling of awe. It was not long before he began to hear stories of the deacon's miserliness and cruelty in regard to financial dealings with the poorer settlers round about. The young minister felt he ought to talk to the man about these reports. But if he offended the man so that he withdrew his support from the church the congregation would no longer be able to support a minister.

Whenever Lionel Fletcher thought about it he was filled with a sick inward fear. One day, however, the young minister was stung into action. He was informed that his deacon held the mortgage over the farm of a poverty-stricken farmer up on the hill, the man could not pay his debts and the deacon intended to seize the property. The farmer was worried sick, because he had nowhere to take his aging wife and delicate child. Lionel Fletcher went

out to visit his deacon on his prosperous farm in
the valley. As he drew near the farmhouse his legs
felt like jelly and he thought he would collapse,
but he went on and knocked at the door. The deacon's wife let him in and sent one of the boys to
bring his father in from the harvest field. As she
made the minister a cup of tea she told him she was
worried about her husband. Of late he had disap-
peared into the bedroom after the midday meal and
when she followed she had found him on his knees.
She had not liked to speak to him about it and she
was afraid he was in some kind of trouble. At the
same time she maintained that he had always been
a good man and of late goodness seemed to shine
from his face. Knowing what he did, Lionel Fletcher
felt more and more unhappy.

Then the man himself arrived. His normal voice
made the windows rattle and now he greeted the
young minister with a tremendous roar of welcome.
Lionel Fletcher felt helpless, but he put up a silent
prayer to God and told the man he was worried
about the farmer on the hill. Knowing the farmer
was in serious financial trouble the young minister
asked his deacon if he knew enough about it to ad-
vise him on how to obtain help. The deacon roared
laughing and said, "You've come to the right man,
Parson. I'll show you in black and white how he

stands." Pulling back a mat he opened a trap-door in the floor and lifted out a deed-box. From this box he produced documents to show that, years before, he had given the man a loan practically as large as the Government valuation of the property. Years had passed and he had repeated the loan, not once, but several times and never had he received a penny in return.

Then he said, "The poor old chap has an obsession that I'm going to close on him and take his property. I don't want his property and I don't want his money. I've told him so a dozen times, but he has this obsession and he regards me as his enemy. I have promised the Lord that I shall see that his wife and child have enough as long as they live and I have made that clear in my will, but I don't want it talked about round this district. It is something between God and me."

As Lionel Fletcher wrote, it was then that he discovered the secret of the radiance in this man's face and later he discovered that there were others he had helped in the same way.

Judge not that ye be not judged. Do not criticize and you will not be criticized. Let us all have the big-mindedness of the Sioux Indian who prayed, "Great Spirit, help me never to judge another man until I have walked two weeks in his moccasins."

The Spirit of Christian magnanimity looks not for the evil in people, but the good in them. This brings us to the second principle we should all lay to heart, "With what measure ye mete it shall be measured to you again." (Matthew vii. 2.)

II

If you are kind to others, they will be kind to you. If you hate others, they will hate you. If you are cheerful, they will be cheerful. If you are gloomy, they will become gloomy. If you love others, they will love you. If you seek the good in others, they will seek the good in you. Furthermore, people become what you think of them. Think of them as mean and they will tend to become mean. Think of them as noble and they tend to rise to your high estimate of them.

Richard Nixon, Vice-President of the United States, faced the great crisis of his career during the campaign for the Presidential elections in 1952. As a young man of thirty-nine he had been chosen by the Republican party as their nominee for the second-highest position in the nation. Then Nixon was accused of wrongfully accepting some thousands of dollars in connection with his political campaign. Immediately there was a nation-wide uproar which threatened extinction to his own political career and disaster for the party he represented. Eventually General Eisenhower suggested that Richard Nixon should appear before the nation on television and over the radio. The decision would be left to the people.

What an immense order for anybody and especially for a young man not long out of the navy! On the way to the studio Richard Nixon went to see his mother, a deeply religious woman, a Quaker. There was one thing he particularly wanted to hear her say and, as they stood on the porch before they parted, she said it, "Son, I'll be thinking of you." That is the Quaker way of saying, "I'll be praying for you." At the studio Richard Nixon asked to be left alone for ten minutes and in that time he prayed.

God led him to look at it this way. The people to whom he would be speaking were all people like himself. He regarded himself as a reasonably decent, kindly individual and he thought of them in the same way. He decided he would just talk to them on that basis, tell them everything, tell them the truth as he would to a friend and he knew they would believe him. With what measure ye mete it shall be measured to you again.

Richard Nixon offered the people honesty, truth, friendship and they responded by the million. Instead of the crisis ending in political disaster for him and his party, it was turned into a tremendous personal and moral victory—and incidentally into a resounding political victory. Treat people decently and they will treat you decently. If you want happiness you must be in a right relationship with your fellow men and women and your God. According to what you give, so will you receive. Happy are the kind-hearted for they will have kindness shown to them. The third truth is this, the man who sows seeds of kindness reaps a continual harvest.

III

It is an extraordinary thing how hungry people are for kindness. I love the story of the minister who went to preach in a country town and was lodged at a small hotel. On the Monday morning he was weary and lonely after an exhausting day. When the waitress asked him what he would have at breakfast he replied, "A boiled egg and a kind word." In due course she returned and placed the egg in front of him. He said, "And what about the kind word?" She replied, "Don't eat the egg."

Not only are people hungry for kindness, but when they receive it they are often transformed. H. M. Stanley, that great man who risked his life to find David Livingstone, was born in poverty. He never knew his father and was disowned by his mother. He grew up in a workhouse and then, as a boy, obtained employment on a Mississippi steamboat. His life was lonely and miserable, till one day he ran away from the boat in New Orleans. That only increased his misery till a kindly gentleman took pity on him, invited him home, washed him, fed him and even embraced him. H. M. Stanley said in after years, "The golden period of my life began from that supreme moment." Blessed indeed are the kind-hearted, because they produce that kind of response.

My first Church was at Port Adelaide, Australia, at the end of the depression. There was still an awful amount of poverty about. I remember going to one house, a mere slum, the front window of which had been smashed in and the hole stuffed with old sacking. The children were dirty and unshod. The drunken parents cared nothing for them. The dirt and the stench were overpowering. I had a deaconess assisting me. She had made friends with one of the girls in this family. She might have judged her as just another urchin of the slums. Instead she saw in her the possibilities which Christ always saw in people and like her Lord she had the gift of evoking those possibilities by the power of kindness and love. This girl responded. She began to take an interest in her appearance and in her studies at school. She became quite a brilliant student and the last I saw of her she was going to the university, training as a teacher. It needed only a little Christian kindness to divert her from a life of crime, drunkenness and immorality into a life of immense value to the community.

Another illustration of the power of kindness is the letter written me by a woman living in St. Leonard's, Sydney, and saying,

"I had a grandchild dying with a serious heart complaint. There was little hope for him when a very kind friend offered to send the child and his parents to America, paying all expenses for a miracle heart operation. He also paid for all medical fees, hospital expenses, and the upkeep of the parents and child while staying in America! Now by the grace of God that same operation is being done with success in Australia.

"However, it was a wonderful blessing from God to us and that kind gentleman was Sir Edward Hallstrom. I would say he was our Good Samaritan as he is to many others.

"Through the love of God, Sir Edward's generous act and the work of these wonderful doctors, I have been inspired to give the rest of my life to God and have given up all worldly pleasures, living for Him only.

"My personal experience is, 'Draw near to God
and He will draw near to you.' Now I want to
live only for God."

All of which brings me to my final thought that
God treats us in the same way. If Jesus warned us
against criticizing others, is He likely to criticize us?
Rather will He see in us the possibilities which He
saw in men like Zaccheus. Others only saw a miserable little grafter, hated and despised by the whole
community. Jesus saw the possibilities in the man
and instead of denouncing his sins, spoke kindly to
him and went to his home to enjoy his hospitality and
offer His own Divine friendship. What a difference
it made to Zaccheus when he responded to the kindness and the love of Christ, and what a difference it
makes to you and me when we respond!

The trouble is we ignore or despise the love of
God. I leave you with another personal experience
of my own to drive home that truth. In Adelaide
one day at a Church gathering a shy little old lady
approached me and said, "My husband passed away
recently. He had some theological books. I wonder
would you like them?" My heart sank as I pictured
some musty, out-of-date tomes. I tried to think of
some excuse, the more so as the address she gave me
was fully sixteen miles from my home and the trip
would involve a whole afternoon. Unable to think

of an excuse in time I promised to go and a week or two later I drove out to the address. When I arrived I found an enormous house in spacious grounds. Remembering the modest appearance and dress of the old lady I presumed that this was some institution or boarding house and I was surprised when she came to the door. "Oh," she said, "you have come about the books. Please follow me." I followed down a long passage, turned left down an even longer one, went through a fernery and came to a separate building which was entirely devoted to her late husband's library. There must have been 20,000 books there. Beautiful statues in white marble and stained-glass windows made me think I was back in an Oxford college. My hostess pointed out the theological section and invited me to help myself. I took away an armful of books, merely leaving a list of what I had taken as she requested. That night she rang up and said, "Mr. Powell, I'm disappointed in you. You hardly took anything. Come back again and bring your friends too." The young ministers of Adelaide, who were all on a stipend of $1400 at that time, had a field day in Mr. James Fowler's library after that.

Now I feel that we treat God as I treated Mrs. Fowler. He offers us happiness and we don't believe Him. God would not command us to be kind-hearted if He were not kind-hearted toward us. His universe is based on love and kindness. Live by that principle and life becomes so much smoother and so much richer. Happy are the kind-hearted for they will have kindness shown to them—by other people and by God.

TONIC CARD

HAPPY ARE THE KIND-HEARTED, FOR THEY WILL HAVE KINDNESS SHOWN TO THEM.

Matthew v. 7 (Phillips).

The good we do today becomes
The happiness of tomorrow.

CHAPTER THREE

POWERFUL HUMILITY

THE THIRD principle of happiness is meekness. "Blessed are the meek, for they shall inherit the earth." We despise meekness, that fawning, snivelling, yes-man attitude which we associate with such unpleasant characters as Uriah Heep, the despicable hypocrite in *David Copperfield*. We picture such people bowing and scraping and we feel the urge to give them a good kick. Surely Jesus did not mean that our happiness as Christians depended on becoming like that!

Certainly not! Jesus himself was never like that although He said, "I am meek and lowly of heart." He was meek, but there was a power about His meekness that frightened some people, especially those who were morally weak or positively evil. No, when Jesus talked about meekness He was talking about something which requires strength; strength of mind, self-control. At the same time it is a habit of mind which draws to it great blessings and makes possible the gift of God's greatest treasures—spiritual peace and moral power.

I remember the Rev. F. W. Boreham preaching on this theme once and pointing out that nowhere is the principle illustrated better than in relation to animals. What animals are multiplying and inheriting the earth? The strong, aggressive animals like lions, tigers, jackals? Not at all. These animals are dying out. The animals which inherit the earth are the gentle, meek, docile animals like sheep, cows, horses, cats. A young mother, recently emigrated to Australia from London and now living near us, was taking her four-year-old boy for a walk. As they passed me, the child said to his mother, "Mummy, what do sheep do? Do they eat anybody? Do they give you rides?" It is precisely because they don't eat people that they are valued and protected. Because they can be tamed and used by men, sheep are multiplying, but our Australian dingoes are being destroyed. Sheep are meek and co-operative, dingoes are not. The Greek word "praos," translated "meek" in our text, is used of animals like horses that have been tamed. Picture a great draught-horse, with muscles rippling, straining at the traces, obedient to the reins. That is meekness in the sense that Jesus uses it.

I

Apply this principle to human beings. Who are those who get on in life; the arrogant, proud, aggressive types, or those who are gentlemanly, kindly, adaptable, cooperative? The French translate our text, "Blessed are the debonair"—meaning "Blessed are the poised, the polite, the well-mannered, the gentlemanly." The aggressive type may appear to forge ahead for a time, but in the long run the gentle people are those who make the real success of life. In speaking of success I am using it in the sense that Jesus meant success, not as the world counts it. The world measures success in terms of money and power over others. Jesus measured success in terms of happiness, inner peace and joy, and the capacity not to dominate others, but to serve them and make them happy.

It is this desire to make others happy which is an essential ingredient of Christian meekness and which, strangely enough, is one of the biggest factors in

making ourselves happy. In reading the life-story of
Lloyd Douglas I was really astonished at his humility
in relation to his publishers. When he wrote his
first novel *Magnificent Obsession* it was rejected
by publisher after publisher. A proud man would
have said, "I'm not going to be insulted any more,"
but Lloyd Douglas was a humble man and he kept
trying others. At last a firm in Chicago accepted his
book and even then, at their command, he had to re-
write pages and pages of it. He had a tendency to
put in too much philosophy and the Christian teaching that he was trying to get across to his readers.
The publishers thought there ought to be more action in the story, more love interest, and back would
come the manuscript. Lloyd Douglas would not
complain, nor would he argue. He would sit down
and meekly re-write sections on which he had spent
months.

Not only that, but he was humble enough to accept suggestions from all kinds of people. That was
how his greatest book began. One day he received a
letter signed by "Hazel McCann," a salesgirl in
Canton, Ohio, asking him if he had ever thought of
what happened to the Robe worn by Christ at the
crucifixion, for which the soldiers had cast lots. Not
only did Lloyd Douglas accept the suggestion, but
he dedicated this book, perhaps the greatest novel

of modern times, to this humble woman. As he began the work of gathering the material he wrote to his publishers saying, "I am itching to get into it; a bit frightened, more than a bit humble, first time I have really been scared in the face of a new job since I wrote the Obsession." Because that was his approach, the approach of meekness and humility, Lloyd Douglas was a successful author. He got on with other people because he considered them. He did not arrogantly force his views on others.

The same is true of many another successful writer. I remember meeting H. V. Morton in Scotland. I was a student at the time. Plenty of others ignored me because I was a youngster. I didn't expect this world-famous author to take any notice of me. But he did. He was one of the humblest men I have ever met. He treated me as his equal, if not his superior. Not once did he express his views. He was intensely interested in me, in Australia, in the work I was doing in Glasgow. Because he was humble he got the very best out of others and when he put it into his books everybody wanted to read them.

The same was true of that delightful cowboy philosopher Will Rogers whose statue stands today outside the door of Congress. Rogers remarked once that he never met a man he did not like. If he had been proud, arrogant, conscious of his success he would have despised others and they would have resented it. But because he was humble he looked up to others. They liked it and loved him for it.

> I have no voice for singing,
>   I cannot make a speech,
> I have no gift for music,
>   I know I cannot teach.
> I am no good at leading,
>   I cannot organize,
> And anything I write
>   Would never win a prize.
>
> It seems my only talent,
>   Is neither big nor rare,
> Just to listen and encourage
>   And to fill a vacant chair.
> But all the gifted people
>   Could not so brightly shine
> Were it not for those who use
>   A talent such as mine.

II

This brings me to my second proposition. You get on better with yourself if you are humble. What are the main sources of unhappiness? There are many, I know, but would you not agree that many people are unhappy today not because they haven't enough to get by, but because the Joneses have more than they have and they can't be happy till they have what the Joneses have? Supposing they could get rid of that pride, and develop Christian humility so that they no longer worry what the Joneses have and rejoice for the Joneses because of their greater possessions. Then this situation would produce not unhappiness, but happiness for them.

Again others are unhappy because people criticize them or pass them by. Their pride is hurt. Christian humility in itself eliminates a considerable amount of criticism. If criticism still comes, then Christian humility accepts it and does something about it. Where pride has been brought under control people are probably not even aware that they are being passed by or if they are, they could not care less. The unhappy people are those who claim some position and are terrified of losing it. Phillips translates our text, "Happy are those who claim nothing, for the whole earth will belong to them." There is a profound truth in that paradox. Selfishly claim position, or privilege or possession and you are terrified all the time of losing them. Develop humility and an indifference to these things and you find you can enjoy the universe without any fear of being deprived of it.

The proud aggressive types are a menace to other people and a menace to themselves. This was proved in an analysis of road accidents made by two Canadian medical men, Doctors W. A. Tillmann and G. E. Hobbs. They took a group of high-accident rate drivers and compared them with an equal group of low-accident rate drivers and studied their personality patterns. A good many factors were involved, of course, but one in particular seemed to stand out in almost every case. The high-accident group consisted of aggressive types, while the low-accident group consisted of drivers who showed consideration for others. These two doctors from Ontario went further and showed that the majority of the aggressive drivers came from unhappy homes, while the considerate, humble people came from normal homes. The aggressive types on the road are killing many innocent people, but they are also killing themselves, leaving the meek, the humble and the considerate to inherit the earth! The meek get on better with themselves so they get on better with other people. They live longer to enjoy the good things of God's physical and spiritual universe.

The Rev. Wylie Blue in his book *Fossicker's Fare* records one of his memories of Lord Kelvin, the great scientist of Glasgow University. For a time Wylie Blue sat as a student in Kelvin's classes. Here is Wylie Blue's own description of the master:

"His discoveries and inventions are almost be-

yond enumeration. Who does not know of his
mariner's compass and of his part in laying the
Atlantic cable? Every field of applied science is
indebted to Kelvin, yet he was so humble. It was
his custom to invite his students, so many at a
time, to his home. I was there one evening when
he called us to listen to the phonograph, the pre-
cursor of the gramophone. We stood around with
the tubes in our ears while Kelvin moved about
ejaculating in his soft voice, 'Wonderful, gentle-
men, wonderful! Some of us have been teaching
the science of sound for many years and we never
knew that from those lines on a cylinder such
words could come.' "

As Wylie Blue points out, it was this sense of wonder,
the attitude of the child, this humility springing
from his Christian faith, which made Kelvin a
learner and an inventor and a great scientist till
his dying day. If he had ceased to be humble he
would have ceased to learn.

III

The third and most important aspect of meekness
and humility is its power to bring us into a right
relationship with God so that not only do we inherit
the earth, but the Kingdom of Heaven, with all its
great spiritual blessings, is ours too. The first beatitude says, "Blessed are the poor in spirit, for theirs

is the Kingdom of Heaven." What does it mean to be poor in spirit? It means the opposite of being high and mighty, proud, aggressive, over-bearing, self-assertive. A man who adopts such an attitude to God cannot receive any blessing from God, because he hasn't started to comprehend what Almighty God is like. The man who finds God and thereby realizes that by comparison he is nothing and has nothing, is poor in spirit. That man is in a right relationship with God and is in a position to have all the spiritual blessings of God poured into his personality. The proud man does not ask and is too proud to accept anyway. The man who is humble enough to be contrite before God, humble enough to ask and to accept God's gifts, is the one to receive them.

Four or five years ago a distinguished professional man in Melbourne asked me as a non-alcoholic "Shepherd" of Alcoholics Anonymous to help his son who was a hopeless alcoholic. The young man had been a brilliant doctor, but the old vicious circle of an unhappy marriage and too much drinking had led to disaster. Normally we did not approach an alcoholic until requested to do so by the patient himself. Too often it led to an antagonism against Alcoholics Anonymous which made effective help later on difficult. However, there were special reasons in this case and I spent an evening with the

alcoholic young doctor. I could make no impression
on him. To start with, he was quite sure he could
control his drinking if he really tried. For another
thing he didn't believe in God and didn't want
God's help. We parted good friends, but I had made
no headway whatever with the main problem because of his inordinate pride. As time passed, he
had another collapse and yet another. He ended up
in jail, not once, but several times. In due course
even his proud spirit was broken and he came to a
meeting of Alcoholics Anonymous and he took the
first step. The first step in A.A. is to admit that your
life is out of control and you are powerless over
alcohol. It takes genuine humility to admit that, but
once that step is taken then it is possible to go on
to the second and find the Power greater than yourself. Then the power of the living God comes upon
the desperate soul and life begins again. "Blessed
are the poor in spirit for theirs is the Kingdom of
Heaven, blessed are the meek for they shall inherit
the earth."

Jesus is always the supreme example of His own
teaching. He was meek, considerate, gentle, yet He
is slowly but surely inheriting the earth. As Napo-
leon Bonaparte put it in his famous statement:
"Alexander, Caesar, Charlemagne and I myself
reared great empires, but upon what do these crea-

tions of our genius depend? Upon force. Jesus alone founded His empire upon love and to this very day millions would die for Him."

Yes, blessed are the meek, for they shall inherit the earth.

TONIC CARD

BLESSED ARE THE MEEK: FOR THEY SHALL INHERIT THE EARTH.

Matthew v. 5.

"Meekness is like one of those fragrant trees which bathes with its perfume the axe that smites into its wood. The meek man gives back love for hate, kindness for unkindness, sweetness for bitterness."

J. R. Miller, D.D.

CHAPTER FOUR

TENSION-DISSOLVING PRAYER

W E COME now to the fourth principle of happiness which I call "Tension-Dissolving Prayer." The text is in Matthew v. 44. "Pray for them which despitefully use you." It is my experience that if we can rise to the point of doing this, then three great blessings follow. In the first place, such a prayer eliminates the burden of tension and depression. Secondly, it eliminates the danger of rash actions because of fear and, thirdly, it eliminates the enemy.

I

I have a friend, rapidly becoming a very dear friend, who happened along to these Wednesday services at a time when life had become a great burden. This man had an enemy who was trying to break him financially and in every other way by legal procedure. It isn't much wonder that the nerves of my friend and his wife began to crack under the strain. The unhappy business dragged on year after year. The prospect seemed entirely dark with no glimmer of hope anywhere.

During the past year or so my friend made the discovery that we don't have to face these things alone. He wrote to me about it saying:

"I have learned that I can do all things through Christ which strengtheneth me. I have taken Jesus into partnership with me in business (which I never dared to do before because I didn't understand that I not only could do so, but should do so). I need hardly say that everything has moved very much more smoothly since, and being the Senior Partner, He has the biggest problems to settle, which He does, because I am now prepared to be led by the hand as a little child. It is not possible to put on paper how much happier I feel since this Partnership started. I have felt the lifting of the yoke and a mental peace that I have never known before. My work is easier to me and, although just as heavy, is a much lighter burden to carry."

That was his first great victory, but there was still the problem of the man who hated him and was seeking to ruin him. My friend came to the vestry one day to talk it over and I would like to use his words again to describe what followed:

"The next point I would like you to know results from our last interview together. You said 'Have you ever thought of praying for the man who has harmed you so much?' I said, 'I have never been able to do it. It would be like praying for the Devil, but I will try.'

"After that interview I started to think on the 'Sermon on the Mount' and the 'Lord's Prayer.' I realized, with a severe shock, that although I had ceased to hate the man who had caused so much misery in our lives and whom I blamed absolutely for my wife's illness—one of the things which made me so bitter toward him—that at the same time I was being a first-class hypocrite each time I said that prayer. I had no right to ask God to forgive me my trespasses unless I was whole-heartedly prepared to do likewise. Ever since that vivid realization I have prayed for all who are persecuting me, particularly the man I hated so much in the past. I am glad I am able to tell you this; because it proved one of the greatest battles of my life. I knew it had to be sincere and not just lip-service. Well I have been able to do so every night since—and sincerely. I feel cleansed of a cancer that has been eating into me for years and which has, I feel sure, done me far more harm than anybody else. I didn't realize what was happening to me. Now I have placed the problem entirely in God's hands. His will be done."

Let us analyze what happens to everybody who prays sincerely for those who despitefully use them. When we have a quarrel we feel angry. If it is a bad quarrel we are consumed with anger. That is an exact description of it. Anger eats us up. It has been well said that many people are ill not because of something they have eaten, but because of something eating them. Americans say that people are burned up with anger. That is true too. Anger uses up, burns up, our spiritual strength and our spiritual resources like a jet aircraft burning up fuel. Our life energy, our life force is diminished by anger and that is why anger leaves us depressed.

The depression is then intensified by other factors. When we hate we are acting against the will of God and the teaching of Christ. Naturally we prefer not to think of that and we repress the thought. That produces a guilt feeling in the unconscious mind and such a feeling always hits back at us, usually in the form of depression. What then can we do? If somebody makes us angry, are we to pretend that we are not angry? We might fool other people, but we can't fool ourselves and we can't fool God. If somebody despitefully uses us and we don't do anything about it, we despise ourselves as spineless and that is depressing. Is there anything we can do about it that will not leave us depressed?

There is only one thing and that is what Jesus said, pray for them that despitefully use you. That will prevent your anger turning into hatred. It will be a constructive response to the stimulus of evil. As Jesus said in this part of the Sermon on the Mount, the Christian faced with a personal enemy should love him, do good to him and pray for him. If you do that it dissolves the tension in your own soul, it prevents anger from consuming your spiritual resources, leaving you depressed, and it paves the way for a spiritual victory which makes you stronger for the trials which may lie ahead. Now let us consider the second benefit which follows when we pray for them that despitefully use us.

II

Affirmative prayer eliminates rash actions due to fear. So often when people quarrel and are driven on by blind anger and hatred they rush into actions which only make things worse. They think up all the horrible things they would like to do to their enemy and what happens? They are immediately filled with fear that their enemy is thinking up the same kind of thing for them. Fear drives people into the most insane kind of activity, which hurts them far more than it hurts their enemy.

Norman Vincent Peale tells of a friend of his who rang him up in a great panic one day. This man, as a boy, had joined a certain firm. The owners of the business liked him, treated him well and he was steadily advanced in the firm until he became sales manager. His panic was caused by the sudden decision of the owners, who were now advanced in age, to sell out to a young, aggressive business man. The sales manager rang Dr. Peale and said: "Things are in a terrible shape. I don't like this new man at all. He is aggressive. He isn't like the men I've been working with. I have heard that he has different sales methods, different accounting methods, different methods of handling customers. I'm not used to these methods. What am I going to do?"

Dr. Peale said to him: "How do you know these methods aren't better than the old ones? One trouble may be that you are thinking of yourself as an old man. Perhaps you are in a rut. Everything may be wonderful under this young man. The thing for you to do is to pray for him and thank the Lord that he had enough money to buy the business. Then thank the Lord that you are there to help him. Send out goodwill thoughts toward him and ask that you may get youthful in your mind again so that you can adopt new ideas."

The sales manager said, "I think he will fire me."

Dr. Peale answered, "On the other hand he may keep you on because you are old and experienced."

That started an argument about whether he was old or not. Eventually he agreed to pray for his new employer. Some days later the sales manager rang Dr. Peale again and said: "You know it worked out just the way you said it would. This man is wonderful. He is going to make this old concern do more business than ever before." The man was quite enthusiastic and happy. Affirmative prayer made all the difference, prayer for the man he feared. Had the fear been allowed to persist he could well have adopted an attitude or done something to offend the new employer and he would have been out in the cold. Pray for them who despitefully use you, and for those you think may so use you, and it will eliminate rashness due to fear.

III

My third truth is that this kind of positive prayer for the enemy will eliminate the enemy. We all want to get rid of our enemies. We would like to kill them, but that's a messy business and the consequences can be awkward! We find it hard just to forget about them and, as I have indicated, to suppress these feelings into the unconscious just means continued depression and nerves. No, the best way to get rid of our enemies is to pray for them.

W. M. Horton records the story of a godly man who, goaded beyond endurance by the persistent malice of an enemy, publicly vowed that he would kill him. It came to the ears of the enemy who waited sardonically to see what the harmless old fool would do. Actually the churchman sought every opportunity to do his enemy good. This greatly amused his enemy at first and then it began to annoy him. One day the enemy's wife was in danger of drowning and the godly man risked his life to save her. The deadlock between the two men was broken at last and the former enemy said: "All right, you've done what you said you would do and I admit it. You have killed me, or at least you have killed the man I was. Now what can I do for you?" If we are to eliminate our enemies we must love them, do them good and begin by praying for them that despitefully use us.

* * *

On a Wednesday afternoon following the lunch hour service a young man rang me up in considerable excitement. He said, "You know how you told us today to pray for those who despitefully use us and in the brief prayer at the end you led us in prayer for those who hate us? Well, at that point I thought of my ex-wife's family. You see, I am divorced and for some reason her people seem to hold me responsible. They have hated me for years. Well, I prayed for them and do you know what happened? A few minutes ago her brother entered the office, came straight over to me and, calling me by my Christian name, held out his hand saying there was no argument between us and he would like to shake hands." This incident had greatly restored the faith of the young man on the phone.

In the weeks that followed there were constant reports from others who found that prayer for people who despitefully used them did release tension in their own souls and lift a burden from them apart from what it did for those who were the object of their prayers.

TONIC CARD

PRAY FOR THEM WHICH DESPITEFULLY USE YOU.

Matthew v. 44.

Getting even with a person means putting yourself on his level.

CHAPTER FIVE

DYING TO LIVE

Jesus said many paradoxical things but surely even He never expressed a more startling paradox than when He said we have to die to live. "He that loseth his life for my sake shall find it." It is a simple principle which runs all through life. Let us study it from three different angles. First, you have to lose in order to win.

I

The farmer has no hope of reaping a harvest unless he takes a whole lot of perfectly good seed and throws it away, burying it in the ground. As Jesus put it

63

(John xii, 24) "Except a corn of wheat fall into the ground and die, it abideth alone; but if it die, it bringeth forth much fruit." The shopkeeper, anxious to make money, has to spend money in order to obtain stock, to provide premises, to make those premises attractive and to advertise his wares. He, too, has to lose in order to win.

To the man with no imagination advertising is sheer waste. It is money down the drain. Such a man would rather hang on to his money and be sure of it, but the man with imagination, courage and the sense of adventure throws money away in advertising in the press, on the radio, on billboards and in a multitude of other ways. One page in one issue of a Sydney newspaper costs over $1,500. A business man in America told me once he had just spent $78,000 on one advertisement in one issue of a well-known magazine and considered it well worth it. Many millions of dollars are thrown away every year in advertising. Yet it pays to advertise. Modern business knows that you have to lose in order to win.

There is another sense in which this is true. Jesus said in the Sermon on the Mount (Matthew v. 30), "If thy right hand offend thee, cut it off and cast it from thee: for it is profitable for thee that one of thy members should perish, and not that thy whole body should be cast into hell." Jesus was using the picturesque hyperbole of the East to drive home His spiritual truth. Pruning is good not only for rose bushes and fruit trees, but also for the human spirit.

The man with an orchard who says, "I'm going for all the fruit I can get; I'm not going to cut any branches off at all," will find that he has far less fruit than the man who reduces the number of branches. So the man who says, "I want to get everything I can from life," finishes up with far less than the man who is prepared to cut things out. Nobody ever enjoyed the ability to play the piano who was not prepared to cut out many other amusements in order to practice and practice and practice. No man is honored as a great surgeon, or judge, or engineer or teacher who was not prepared to "scorn delights and live laborious days" as Milton put it. You must lose in order to win.

This same principle applies to the greatest blessings of the spiritual life. Some years ago in Adelaide, I was holidaying in the Mount Lofty Ranges high above that city. I went for a walk one day to the look-out on the peak of Mt. Lofty. On the way I passed an old and picturesque Church of England, the Church of the Epiphany. It stands beside the highway, set amid some ancient English trees. The whole atmosphere was one of peace and security, something which is always pleasant, and which meant much to me at the time because it was early in the war and the news was far from good. I decided to slip into the church and have a brief time of meditation and prayer. As I knelt there I felt the peace of God stealing upon my soul. I felt I was being strengthened. As I looked up I noticed that the Bible was open on the lectern and it occurred to me that there might be a message for me on that open page. I walked to the lectern, but a sense of disappointment came to me as I read the words that first struck my eye. The Bible was open at the last chapter of the book of Jonah and the story concerned the argument between that reluctant prophet and the Lord over his duty to the wicked city of Nineveh. The words seemed to have no connection whatever with my feeling of spiritual elation and inward peace.

I left the church and continued my walk to the top of Mt. Lofty. Then as I looked down over the city of Adelaide and drank in that magnificent vista which includes so much of the coast of South Australia, there came back to me the last verse of the book of Jonah, the words of God, "Should not I spare Nineveh, that great city, wherein are more than six-score thousand persons that cannot discern between their right hand and their left hand; and also much cattle." I felt then that I understood the message God meant me to take from the open Bible. I had gone into that church seeking to get—to get spiritual peace and strength for myself. That is all right, but if you want to keep these things, you must give them away. You must be concerned about the great city and all those who likewise need spiritual peace and strength. Try to hang on to your spiritual blessings for yourself and they soon evaporate. Share them with others, give them away and they are multiplied to you.

II

Let us consider the truth that you have to lose yourself in order to find yourself from a second angle. Take any great personality. Are they not most truly themselves when utterly forgetful of self and absorbed in some great task? It was said of Michelangelo that, after weeks of working upon his great statue of David, his face glowed. He seemed a bigger and a grander person. At the beginning of this century, a school of philosophy led by Bosanquet and calling themselves the Idealists based their whole thinking on this truth. They believed that each of us has an ideal self which can be realized when we become utterly absorbed in some great purpose. The selfish who are absorbed with themselves, who are for ever feeling their own physical and spiritual pulses, are the unhappiest people on earth. They continually shrivel in soul. But those who can forget self in something beyond self are the ones who find the blessedness which Jesus knew.

Here is a letter written by a woman living in a North Shore suburb of Sydney:

October 12th, 1953

"Dear Sir,

"I would like to tell you of my own experience. Some years ago I lost, after serious illness, both my husband and only daughter (a beautiful girl of twenty-four) in the space of a few months. Both had long lingering illnesses and I was left a nervous wreck, thoroughly exhausted mentally and spiritually. The finances were exhausted too. I had two lads, one a young apprentice and the other a schoolboy. Neither was able to support himself.

"As I sat in mental despair I realized that the boys, too, must have had a terrific nervous strain. I decided to give them just what I was needing. There was no money for holidays. I could only use what was around me.

"I set the meals a bit nicer, took extra care with the cooking, made their bedrooms more comfortable, brought curtains and extras from other parts of the house to give them extra comfort and generally build up the atmosphere of the home. Boy-like they just accepted it and if they noticed it or appreciated it at all, it was just passed off as 'Good.'

"But, sir, I was the one that benefitted. I proved to the full measure the text, 'He that loseth his life shall find it.' In losing my life to all their need, I saved my own. I came out of it all with balance and strength. I was able, after awhile, to take my place once more in the world. People thought I had got over it very quickly. No, sir, I never got over it, but the simple Christian teachings of the Sermon on the Mount stood by me in desperate days and proved to me that it is the true remedy for all ills. After all, Jesus' injunction in dealing with ills of mankind was: 'Rise, take up thy bed and walk,' which is our way of saying, 'Stand on your two feet, shoulder your responsibilities and get a move on.'

"I am sending my name and address as proof of my sincerity and truth, but please keep me anonymous. I only want to help someone else who is looking for the formula for better living."

III

We come now to the third and most difficult aspect to understand. It is easy enough to understand that we have to lose before we can win. We can agree that those who lose themselves in some absorbing task or some great ideal find their true selves and an inner harmony which makes for happiness. It is not so easy to see how actual dying is necessary for life.

In my church at Port Adelaide were two people who had migrated from Scotland at the beginning of the depression. They had a most dreadful battle for survival. The one joy of their life was their only child, a boy who was admired and beloved by all who knew him. Early in the war this boy enlisted in the Air Force. One day came the tragic news that he had been lost in air operations over Europe. I dreaded to meet them. I thought they would be completely shattered. Instead I found them magnificent. Their attitude was, "Our boy died for a free and better world. All right, we will live for it." Others have been so inspired by their spirit that many lives are the better. I don't think it is too much to say that in the light of eternity that boy's short life will contribute more to the well-being of mankind than if he had lived to be a hundred.

Again, I think of the manner in which Temple Hospital and Temple University were built in Philadelphia. According to the record their founder was Russell Conwell. But their real founder was Johnny Ring, who died before either the hospital or university had ever been conceived. Johnny was a fellow student with Conwell at the time when Conwell was an unbeliever, but Johnny was an ardent Christian and stood up to the taunts of Conwell and others when he read his Bible and said his prayers. Ring and Conwell went off to the Civil War together. Surprised by the enemy, their company was driven back across a bridge and Conwell was distressed to find that he had dropped his sword during his flight. Their men had already set fire to the bridge, but Johnny Ring volunteered to run back for the sword. In doing so he was badly burned and he died in Russell Conwell's arms a few days later.

Conwell was so impressed by his Christian faith and courage that he was converted and vowed that he would live two lives, one for Johnny Ring and one for himself. He devoted both lives to the creation of Temple Hospital and Temple University and he did so by touring America giving the most famous lecture of the century. It was called "Acres of Diamonds." It was delivered so often that in the end it was equivalent to a nightly lecture without interruption for fifteen years. It raised the equivalent of $8,-000,000 and it gave a university education to hundreds who would have been denied such an education otherwise. "Except a corn of wheat fall into the ground and die it abideth alone, but if it die it bringeth forth much fruit."

We may not consciously notice war memorials when we pass them, but they must affect us unconsciously and surely the reminder of so many who laid down their lives for us is a challenge to nobler living. If that is true of ordinary human beings, how much more true it is of Jesus Christ upon the Cross. Think of the saving power of the Cross in the lives of men and women.

Now let us take this principle a stage further. It has been said that the blood of the martyrs is the seed of the Church. That is proving true even at this very moment. For some time I have been deeply concerned by the state of affairs in a certain Central

American republic. Things are primitive there and for a long time there has been active persecution of the Protestant Church. In the last five years forty-two church buildings have been completely destroyed. 110 primary schools have been closed. Fifty-one Protestants have been murdered. In the light of such persecution and Government frustration one would expect to hear that the Protestants were prepared to give up. What are the facts? In the past five years the Protestant membership has increased 51 per cent. The Church which is prepared to lose its life shall find it.

All these things apply to the world. Jesus used the words in connection with Himself and His death on the Cross. We believe that in the light of eternity we shall understand just what He meant and shall give God glory to find that death is not tragedy, but the gateway to the real life beyond, the life which we cannot enter until we are prepared to release our hold on physical life in this world.

I think we may sum it all up by quoting a distinguished scientist, an eminent American geologist who, during a public lecture, made the statement that there is an Administration back of the Universe which conserves its spiritual and personal values. A questioner asked him, "How can you say there is a trustworthy Divine Administrator who guarantees the permanence of spiritual values when a personality like Jesus suffered defeat?"

The scientist replied, "In the light of what Jesus accomplished during His days on earth and in the centuries since, do you really think Jesus was defeated?"

TONIC CARD

HE THAT LOSETH HIS LIFE FOR MY SAKE SHALL FIND IT.

Matthew x. 39.

The measure of a life, after all, is not its duration, but its donation. How much will you be missed?

Peter Marshall.

CHAPTER SIX

TRUSTING GOD DAILY

I T WAS ON March 14th, 1948, that I issued my first tonic prayer card in the Collins Street Independent Church, Melbourne, Australia. In that church we issued them monthly and the practice is still being maintained there. In St. Stephen's we issue them weekly. In five years the grand total has passed the third of a million mark. In that time and with such a mass of cards (costing, incidentally, about $6,000) we have had many reports and we have learned many lessons.

One of the things we learned was that the card which helped the most people was the one based on the text, "I will fear no evil, for Thou art with me."

Another card which is still in constant demand is the one with the serenity prayer, "God grant me the serenity to accept the things I cannot change, courage to change the things I can and wisdom to know the difference."

A card which had a spectacular influence in many lives was based on the text, "This is the day which the Lord hath made; we will rejoice and be glad in it." It was a card teaching this principle of trusting God daily. Here is a letter describing its influence in one life. The writer lives in Manly, N.S.W. The letter is dated, October 10th, 1953.

"I feel I must share my blessings with others and so fulfil the law of Christ. For many years prior to attending the mid-week services I suffered from insomnia and could never hope for a natural night's sleep. I therefore took large doses of sleeping drugs. These became such a habit that I never thought I would ever have a night's sleep without first taking them.

"On the night after attending the tonic card address on the subject, 'Live One Day at a Time,' I slept right through the night and awoke in the morning, refreshed and ready for many heavy duties that awaited me. Since then I have given up taking the sleeping drugs and have never had to resort to them again. In fact my sleep has been so excellent that at about 9 P.M. I am ready to go to bed and to sleep. I know that the tonic I received could never be bought because it is the gift of God."

The principles of happiness as taught by Jesus would not be complete without His important precept in this regard, "Be not anxious for the morrow" (Matthew vi. 34. R.V.). In dealing with this principle, I want you to bear in mind three key words, *detachment, acceptance,* and *trust.*

1

The other day I was having a game of golf with a man who has reached the very top in the banking world. Now I should think that a man who holds a responsible position in a bank must have many grave decisions to make and a heavy burden of worry in consequence. My friend surprised me by saying that he could not understand people who took their business worries home with them. He had cultivated the art of leaving all that behind him when he left the office. He might, on waking in the morning, mull over the terms of a letter which he would have to dictate later to his general manager, but he did not regard that as a worry. He refused to wear himself out emotionally by fretting over these things all night. He watched other men taking home bags of work and he would ask them how they expected to arrive fresh for work in the morning. He was at the top because he had learned to live one day at a time by taking Christ literally, "Be not anxious for the morrow."

I asked him how he had developed this detached attitude. He agreed that it was probably his early training as a bank clerk. As you know most banks close at 3 P.M. so that each day's business can be completed and nothing left over to the morrow. The good banker does not carry over a burden of work from yesterday, nor does he have to use up emotional resources worrying about today's work which he will have to push on to the morrow. He does each day's work today and, doing that, is much more efficient and serene. I then asked my friend how he coped with the big decisions which he constantly had to make—decisions which often meant great happiness or misery to the clients approaching him. He felt that it was a question of intellectual and moral integrity. He came at every decision in the light of the principles which should guide us all. He would not stretch his conscience to favor one man or handicap another. He would give his very best concentrated thought to every problem and, having done his best, he put it out of his mind, went home, had a good dinner and a good sleep. Today he is one of the most successful, most honored and most respected men in Sydney.

That is a man's story. Now let me give you a woman's story to remind us of the importance of living one day at a time, detached from the shadow of the past and detached from fear of the future. Dale Carnegie, when he wrote his book on *How to Stop Worrying and Start Living,* thought this principle so important that in all the thirty chapters in his book he made the chapter entitled "Live in Day-Tight Compartments" the first.

He concludes that chapter with a story. Mrs. E. K. Shields of Saginaw, Michigan, a city I know well, lost her husband. She was left lonely, grief-stricken and poverty-stricken. Her sense of depression was so great she would have committed suicide had it not been for the grief it would have brought to her sister. She had to earn her living and she set out to sell books to country schools. She needed a car to do this and put almost all she had on the deposit for a used one. She became more and more depressed. Business was bad. She began to lie awake at night wondering how she could meet the next installment on the car, worrying what would happen to her if she fell sick, how she could pay for her room. She had nothing to live for and dreaded getting up each morning. Then one day she read a sentence which changed her life.

It said, "Every day is a new life to a wise man." She pasted that sentence to the windshield. She repeated that positive thought until it drove all the negative thoughts from her mind. She now reports that she is happy, fairly successful, with plenty of enthusiasm and love for life. "Every day is a new life to a wise man."

II

While I was typing the above paragraph, a friend rang to say that her husband, in the prime of life, had been found to have serious heart trouble. This family has had many battles to fight, many burdens to carry and I was not surprised that my friend's heart had collapsed under the strain. You can imagine the blow it must have been. In telling me of it his wife said something which I thought most significant: "The blow seemed overwhelming and I was worried sick until Saturday morning when I suddenly realized that my worry was not going to alter the situation except for the worse. I had better accept the situation and adjust my life accordingly. It gives me a pain to look at the garden and think that I'll never have his help in it again. But after all he is still with us and with proper treatment he should be able to keep going indefinitely." What a different atmosphere was born in her soul and in that home when she was prepared to accept a situation which could not be changed by worrying about it.

A few minutes after this telephone conversation, I was shown a letter written to somebody else which described the influence of a tonic prayer card produced by my colleague and successor in Melbourne. It contained the two words, "Forget it." The writer of the letter said,

> "I found it most helpful and we sent it to a friend in England who was very badly in need of spiritual help. From a note received from her lately it has done more for her than anything else. Her faith is being restored and we do want to follow up that card with others."

I would say that a big proportion of most worry is the refusal to accept what is past and to accept what is true and unchangeable as far as the present and future are concerned. Do you remember the story of Willis H. Carrier, the biggest man in the air-conditioning industry? Years ago, as a young man, he worked for the Buffalo Forge Company, in Buffalo, New York. They sent him to install a gas-cleaning device in a plate-glass factory in Missouri. The device, which cost $20,000, was still in the experimental stage and young Carrier met with many unexpected difficulties. If he had succeeded, he would have been made for life. But instead he faced utter and dreadful failure. The machine worked after a fashion, but not well enough to meet the guarantee. He wrote: "I was stunned by my failure. My stomach, my insides began to twist and turn. For awhile I was so worried I couldn't sleep."

In time, his common sense told him worry wasn't getting him anywhere. He took three steps which saved the day. First he analyzed the situation fearlessly and honestly, figuring what was the worst that could possibly happen because of this failure. He realized that he would not be jailed or shot. He could have been dismissed, but there were other jobs. Having faced the worst that could happen, he reconciled himself to accept it if it came. His employers might lose $20,000, but the machine was experimental anyway and they could afford to charge it to research. Then he found that his mind was no longer clouded with worry. No longer was it paralyzed with fear. He could think. As he thought, he saw that by spending another $5,000 he might make the machine work properly. He did so, made his reputation and enabled his firm, instead of losing $20,000, to make a very handsome profit.

Analyze your worry calmly. You will find so much of it is refusal to accept something that can't be altered in the past, or refusal to accept something unpleasant in the present, or possibly in the future.

Accept facts, accept the forgiveness of God and so break free from the burden of the past and the burden of the future.

III

The third and most important thing is trust. Many people believe in God, but they don't trust him in a practical manner. Not long ago a business man was showing me his Bible. It has been his practice for many years to mark texts which appeal to him and especially texts which have helped him in some great crises. I noticed in the margin, against 1st Kings vi. 13, "War news is as black as appears possible." The date was June 17th, 1940. This man, like many other people, was worried sick because the news had leaked out that France was about to capitulate to Hitler. Turning to his Bible, he lighted upon the words, "I will dwell among the children of Israel, and will not forsake my people, Israel." Here was the word of God to this man, "I will not forsake my people." That faith steadied him then.

A few weeks ago, in the heart of Sydney, he had one of those days when everything seemed to go wrong and he himself got all snarled up inside. You know how it is. As he put it: "I became negative. I know it now. I failed to call for God's help when I should have done. I was too wrapped up in what was

happening. I slipped badly as a Christian and paid
for it all day. On the ferry home, I at last awakened
to what I should have done earlier." As soon as he
reached his house, he went to a quiet spot and got
things right with God. Next morning, he started out
trusting in God with a positive mind, telling himself,
"This is the day which the Lord hath made, we will
rejoice and be glad in it." Because he trusted in God
he was free and relaxed and happy all day.

If God brought us through the war, He can bring
us safely through the problems of today. But how
many of us trust Him! How many of us open our
souls to His power in the day-to-day problems and
perplexities of life?

We all need a daily reminder of the ever-present
power of God to help and bless. I would like to see
many more firms and factories do what the *Dallas
News* does in America. They begin every day with a
prayer meeting for both management and staff.
Would it make any difference to your firm or department if that were done? It might be hard to or-
ganize, but each one of us can do it in his own private
life. Begin the day by reminding yourself to trust
God.

I remember another experience associated with
the card on which we printed the text I have just
quoted, "This is the day which the Lord hath made,

we will rejoice and be glad in it." On the bottom of the card we had printed the prayer you will find at the end of this chapter. It so happened that the card came into the hands of an elderly gentleman who was facing a major operation, who knew that his chances of survival were slim and who was so depressed about it he didn't really care if he did survive or not. But a friend gave him this card and both before and after the operation he kept repeating this prayer,

> Every day and every hour,
> Father, I breathe in Thy life-giving power—
> Power to love, power to be pure,
> Power to be well, power to endure.

The change in the old man was absolutely remarkable. For years he had been struggling along on half power. Now he really began to live again. Every day and every hour, trusting in God his Father, he breathed in power.

That is the basis of the whole thing, isn't it? When Jesus said, "Be not anxious for the morrow," it was in no flippant or irresponsible spirit that He spoke. He based it all on a practical trust in the Fatherhood of God. That was His answer to the problem of worry. You will find His cure for it all there in the sixth chapter of Matthew. As He saw it, worry is unnecessary because God knows and God cares. He gave us life and He will sustain it. He made the body and He will clothe it. He looks after the flowers and the birds. He will look after you. Again, Jesus taught that worry is not only unnecessary but futile. It achieves nothing and escapes nothing. Finally He taught that worry is dangerous because it conflicts with single-hearted concentration on the Kingdom of God and our highest welfare. Either you believe in the love of God or you don't. If you don't, you will, sooner or later, face disillusionment and depression. If you do, you can face life one day at a time and win the victory that He makes possible.

May I leave this last thought with you? Jesus said that faith could remove mountains. That sounds an exaggeration, but put it in mental and spiritual terms. Many of us have mountains in the mind, mountains of worry, mountains of fear, mountains of sorrow, mountains of anxiety. Those mountains can overwhelm us. They can paralyze us when we have not faith. But where there is faith that we can remove them, we go to work on the mountains. Bit by bit we carry them away. Day by day, yes, one day at a time, the mountain is removed. It is removed into the sea. Why the sea? Because that was the Bible way of saying it was finally and completely destroyed.

Your mountain of worry can be removed for ever

if you can learn detachment, acceptance and trust—
and the greatest of these is trust. Therefore I say, "Be
not anxious for the morrow."

TONIC CARD

BE NOT ANXIOUS FOR THE MORROW.
Matthew vi. 34 (R.V.)

Every day and every hour
Father, I breathe in Thy life-giving power—
Power to love, power to be pure,
Power to be well, power to endure.

CHAPTER SEVEN

CHANGING THE TARGET

WHAT DO YOU want from life? If you could have anything at all what would you choose? Wealth? Happiness? Love? Health? Peace of Mind? Power? Honor? Fame? Success? Let us pause for a moment and choose what we want before we go on . . .

In the light of the choice we have made, let us listen again to the words of Jesus in Matthew vi. 33, "Seek ye first the Kingdom of God, and His righteousness and all these things shall be added unto you." Jesus did not say we could not have these other things, but He did say that if we want them we have to aim at something else. We have to cnange our target. It seems paradoxical, indeed it seems plain silly, to say that if you want something badly the best thing you can do is to aim at something else. Yet consider how truly this principle does apply to life in three different directions: wealth, happiness, self.

I

Aim at wealth as your main object in life and you will get it, but it will do you no good. Set your heart upon the Kingdom of God and wealth may come to you, but you couldn't care less because you will have all that money is supposed to buy and doesn't—happiness, harmony, love, peace of mind.

All of us, I suppose, have some object in life. We are so made that this object becomes more and more an obsession with us. It gets such a grip on us that we are enslaved to it. If it is an unworthy object it will wither the personality. If it is a noble object it will lift us up and make us great.

In 1953, Harrison Williams died, having spent most of his life trying to build a fortune of 1,000 million dollars. Born in Ohio, he was an ambitious young man. At nineteen he was running a tricycle factory. Going to New York, he entered the tire business at the beginning of the automotive age and made his first fortune. He then got in on the ground floor of the electric power boom. At one stage, Harrison Williams controlled one-sixth of all the public utilities in the country. He acquired $680,000,000 and would have reached his ambition of making his a round billion dollars but for the Wall Street crash in 1929. At the point when he reached $680,000,000 somebody asked Harrison Williams why he didn't quit. He said he couldn't because he wanted to make it a round billion.

That is how money becomes an obsession with people. When they have far more than they can possibly use they still have to go on. No wonder Andrew Carnegie, another multi-millionaire, said, "I know few millionaires who smile." A Vanderbilt who had a fortune worth $300,000,000 said: "Such wealth as mine is too heavy a burden for any man to bear. The weight of it is crushing me and killing me. I have no pleasure in it and no use for it."

In the play, *Edward My Son,* we have the picture of a man, beginning in humble circumstances who was determined to make money by hook or by crook. He sacrificed his friends in order to get it. He stooped to arson to benefit from insurance. To get what he wanted from then on he used money. He was even prepared to purchase a school to make sure that his son was not expelled from it. It isn't any wonder that his son went wrong and his wife's nerves collapsed and she took to drink. The one fine thing the boy did was to enlist in the Air Force. Then he died in the Battle for Britain. At the end Edward's

rather was left with his wealth—alone, desolate, trying to find somewhere to escape from his misery.

That was fiction, but there was nothing fictional
about a man I knew. Perhaps he was not so unscru-
pulous and perhaps his son did not die in the Battle
for Britain. But it was the same dreary story. Money
was the one great object of his life. He was only interested in friends if they could help him to make
more money. He was mean with his family and then
he was foolish with them, lavishing gifts on them to
win back the affection he knew he had lost. He began to suspect them of looking forward to his death
so that they could divide up his fortune. It was my
duty to call on him from time to time. It was certainly never a pleasure. He was full of complaints—
about the government, the dreadful state of the country, the weather and the gardener and everybody
and everything else. Make wealth the object of your
life; you will get it, but it will do you no good.

It was said of Harrison Williams, as of others, that
"He had the Midas touch." People use this expression as a term of envy. Everything you touch turns
to gold. But the Midas story was invented as a warning and we do well to heed that warning. Midas,
King of Lydia, according to the quaint belief of the
ancients, did a favor for the god Bacchus who invited him to name any wish he liked. He wished
that all he touched should immediately be turned to

gold. Finding the power given him, Midas rushed round turning his whole palace into gold. In wild excitement, he ordered the greatest banquet in history to celebrate his good fortune. Then, as he lifted the food and wine to his lips it all became gold. At last, starving and wretched amid his wealth, he cast himself at the feet of Bacchus and pleaded with him to take back his gift.

Wealth is a means to an end and, if we become obsessed with the means, we are in danger of missing the end. To become obsessed with money is to become obsessed with something beneath personality. We belittle ourselves when we give ourselves to money. Why do we want money anyway? Is it not to purchase that which will make us happy? Jesus pointed us to the truer and surer path to happiness. He said, "Seek ye first the Kingdom of God and His righteousness and all these things shall be added unto you." Phillips translates that, "Set your heart upon His Kingdom and His goodness and all these things will come to you as a matter of course."

How does it work? The Kingdom of God is where God is King, where Jesus Christ is Lord. Applying it to our own lives, it means that in place of our own will, which is ill-formed and warped by all kinds of petty, unworthy instincts and impulses, we are guided by the all-wise and all-loving will of God. The point that so many fail to realize is that God's will is never for our disadvantage or hurt, but always for our highest and eternal welfare. If we try to run our own lives we meet frustration, distraction, disintegration, disharmony, nerves and collapse. Seek God's will and you will find integration of personality, harmony, happiness and all the other wonderful things that money can never buy. Seek ye first the Kingdom of God, make God king, and all these things shall be added unto you.

II

Make happiness your main aim in life and you won't keep it. Set your heart upon the Kingdom of God and you will find happiness as the inevitable by-product.

Anybody who has read any philosophy at all knows all about the hedonistic paradox. Those who seek happiness don't find it. Those who look for something else often discover happiness. Now, of course, this doctrine needs to be properly understood. I think of a young lady who is crazy about ice-skating. She goes skating to enjoy herself and she does enjoy herself. She seeks happiness and she finds it. I think of a man who loves sailing in the harbor. He goes out to enjoy himself and he does enjoy himself. But the point is this: if the young lady did nothing else day after day, skating would soon begin to pall. If the man in his yacht did nothing else, he would go to seed. Further, if they begin to ask themselves whether they are enjoying themselves, if they begin to worry whether they are happy or not, they soon find there is something wrong. It is when they lose themselves in doing something which appeals to them and forget themselves that they are happy.

Happy are those who can become absorbed in their daily work as a worthwhile occupation. If that work can contribute to the Kingdom of God in this world, if they themselves are fitted for it and if within themselves they have become well-adjusted personalities because God's will prevails in them, they are the Happy Warriors. They are not aiming primarily at happiness, they are aiming to do a worthwhile job in life and, by seeking first the Kingdom of God, happiness has been added. Wealth, happiness and all the rest are additions by God to those who seek first His Kingdom and His righteousness.

One day, at a home for aged ladies, a colleague was speaking and asked the assembled people to note the neatness and beauty of the gardens. He said that the heavy work of digging and mowing the lawn was done by a paid gardener, but all the rest was done by two old ladies, both well over eighty and one nearly ninety. They rejoiced to keep the gardens neat and tidy, to care for the flowers and do all the other things needed. He asked these two to stand up. As he said, it was just lovely to see them, a wonderful old pair, so happy at this piece of service. There are some who sit about thinking how unhappy they are, full of self-pity, moaning because their relatives don't come to see them and listen to all their complaints. They are obsessed with self. The others are obsessed with the garden. To them has been added health and happiness.

III

One of the worst things that can happen to most people is to be left entirely to themselves. If we really want to punish a criminal we put him in solitary confinement. When people go out of their mind we say they are "beside themselves." Ibsen drove home the terrible punishment meted out to the self-centered in his play *Peer Gynt*. He makes the superintendent of an asylum say: "It's here that men are most themselves—themselves and nothing but themselves. Each shuts himself in a cask of self. None has a tear for others' woes or cares what any other thinks." One would not apply such terrible words to all unhappy inmates of mental hospitals, but medical authorities assure me that in regard to severe cases there is much truth in the assertion that the end of obsession with self is madness and misery.

How different it is if we seek first the Kingdom of God in our own lives. We can't do that without caring for others and seeking to build the Kingdom of God in the whole community. Go into an Eastern city where the people have never heard of the Kingdom of God, a city like Bagdad or Benares, as I have been. What do you find? Everyone is an individualist, pushing his own self-interest. Down the narrow streets there are no traffic laws, no consideration for others. People jostle and shout and scream. It is each man for himself and everybody is held up. There is no progress. Traffic laws are an elementary application of the Kingdom of God to human society. It is a systematizing of consideration for others and so everybody benefits. The selfish man who defies the traffic laws brings trouble to others and to himself. When each individual seeks the welfare of the whole community everybody prospers. Wealth and happiness are added.

Stanley Jones has a chapter entitled, "The Self-centered are the Self-disrupted," and quotes two examples of what he means. A child travelling second class on a steamer was playing ball. Her ball rolled through the barrier into the first class section and she ran in to retrieve it. A girl in the first class snarled at her, "You get back on your own side, you common little child." By saying that she hurt the other child, but she also hurt herself. As Stanley

Jones remarked, the look on her face showed she
was disrupted in her personality. She was at war
with herself. One half of her was saying, "Aren't
you ashamed of yourself?" The other half was trying to justify her snobbishness. When we seek first
the Kingdom of God there is no such disruption of
personality.

In the same way, Stanley Jones describes an Englishman in the Indian Civil Service. He was utterly
self-centered and beaten by it. His health went to
pieces. He loathed India and the Indians. He yearned
for the day when he could take his pension and get
out of it all. Then he came to see himself as the
center of the trouble. He made self-surrender to
the will of God. He began to seek first the Kingdom
of God. Instead of making himself the center of the
universe, he saw God as the center. Instead of life
being "eccentric" or "off-center," it now came into
harmony. The Englishman found health of body,
mind and soul. He loves Indians and India and
both have responded with their love. He has become
creative, so much so that he was sent to the north-
west frontier to create goodwill, the place where
there is a greater need of goodwill than anywhere
else on earth. Before, he was like a fly-wheel out of
its true bearings, threatening to shake itself and
the whole factory to pieces. Now the fly-wheel is on

its true center revolving with rhythm, power and constructive energy.

One Saturday evening in Freiburg the old cathedral organist was practicing, in preparation for Sunday. A younger man came in, listened for awhile and then asked permission to play the organ. The old man was jealous of his instrument and refused. The younger man persisted and at last, most reluctantly, the old organist gave his consent. In a moment the most glorious music echoed round the cathedral. The local organist listened enraptured and, at the end, said, "Excuse me, what is your name?"

The stranger replied, "My name is Mendelssohn."

Why not let the Master take over your life?

TONIC CARD

SEEK YE FIRST THE KINGDOM OF GOD,
AND HIS RIGHTEOUSNESS;
AND ALL THESE THINGS SHALL BE
ADDED UNTO YOU.

Matthew vi. 33.

The surest steps towards happiness
are the church steps.

CHAPTER EIGHT

DOING WHAT YOU LIKE

Most people, I suppose, would say that they would be perfectly happy if they could do what they liked. Now the happiness that Christ offers is precisely that happiness, provided that we follow Him and learn to like that which will make us really happy, that which ministers to the true welfare of ourselves and others. "I am the Truth" said Jesus. "The Truth shall make you free." In the eighth chapter of John, Jesus went on to say, "Everyone who commits sin is a slave" (as Moffatt translates it). Then He said, "If the Son shall make you free, ye shall be free indeed." I want you to consider two propositions based on that truth.

I

There is no slavery like the slavery of sin. It has been well said that people who do what they like, do not like what they do. People who do as they please, are seldom pleased with what they do. People who center themselves on themselves, come to dislike the self which they have put at the center. Express yourself and you will soon not like the self you are expressing. Hence the boredom of the worldly and the selfish.

I have referred already to my deaconess at Port Adelaide, a woman worth her weight in gold. She used to give considerable time to a large family living in wretched circumstances. One of the boys began to earn money and it was hoped that his income would help to drive away the spectre of want and misery that everlastingly haunted their home. Unfortunately he was a boy with a firm conviction that the greatest thing in life was to be able to do what you like. One night he did and ended up in jail. When he was due to come out of jail, the deaconess came to me to discuss how we could give him an entirely new start in life. We decided to send him right away to another part of the state, away from his old associates, where people did not know him and where a farmer promised to give him a chance. He went off promising us that he would not slip again. You could see that he was sincere, but there is no slavery like the slavery of sin. The unfortunate circumstances of his childhood and his own wrong thinking had built up in that boy a compulsion to steal and he could not help himself. In less than a week he was in trouble again.

Once I saw a group of church young men and women befriend a boy whose compulsion towards gambling had led him into trouble. They went the second and the third mile with this young man, but his compulsion to gambling, his slavery to sin, was such that he too ended up in jail. When he came out, the minister of another church, who is specially trained in this sort of work, welcomed him, found him accommodation and got him a job. In less than a week he was gambling again and back in all the strife in the world. There is no slavery like the slavery of sin.

I thing of J. B. Priestley's powerful story of a perfectly respectable business man who had a weakness for loose women. He knew that it was dragging him down, that one day it would destroy his reputation and ruin everything. Again and again, he told himself he had sinned for the last time. Then a few days later he would feel the urge, the compulsion, coming on again and he knew that inevitably he would fall.

How many times have I dealt with compulsive

alcoholics who were quite sure they had had their last drink! The most recent drinking bout had brought such misery they were positive they were finished with it for ever. Yet again the craving would return and in their hearts they knew they would fall in spite of all the appalling consequences. In fact, that feeling precipitated the disaster. They told themselves it was inevitable so what was the use of struggling?

Earlier we were considering those who were money-mad, people obsessed with the passion for wealth. Wealth seems to grip, to enslave the mind and the spirit, until they can think of nothing else. The love of money drags them further and further down till their souls are withered and there is no real satisfaction left in life for them at all. All these and many others too are slaves to sin. They do what they like and then they don't like what they do, but they cannot give it up. "O wretched man that I am," cried the Apostle Paul, faced with this problem, "who will deliver me from the body of this death? I thank God through Jesus Christ our Lord." J. B. Phillips paraphrases the familiar words of the Authorized Version: "It is an agonizing situation, and who on earth can set me free from the clutches of my own sinful nature? I thank God there is a way out through Jesus Christ our Lord."

What is the way out through Jesus Christ?

II

There is no liberty like the liberty of Christ. Jesus said, "If the Son shall make you free, ye shall be free indeed." How does Jesus set us free? It is my conviction that He does so in two ways. First, by breaking the power of sin in our personalties and, secondly, by leading us into the life which is so satisfying that we are no longer tempted to turn aside into wrong and unsatisfying bypaths.

(a) *Liberty from the Compulsion of Sin.* In the great majority of those who have a compulsion to steal, or to gamble, to indulge in sex or alcohol, or lust after money or anything else it seems to me that there is an unsatisfied soul, a soul that is hungry for love. Because they are not properly adjusted and satisfied at the heart of them, these people become all "snarled up" inside until they don't know what they want. They begin to lash out at others. They become anti-social. Because they don't keep the law, society punishes them and they become more anti-social than ever. More punishment follows and the problem becomes worse and worse.

A feature of these unhappy people with inner compulsions to sin is frequently a great fear. It may be fear of punishment, fear of exposure, fear of the future, or just a blind fear which they cannot identify, but which certainly intensifies greatly the tension at the heart of them. Bit by bit this tension goes on building up until they are compelled, even against their better judgment and will, to do something they know they shouldn't. I am convinced that tension is the main problem and if we can eliminate that while strengthening the right desires inside a man, then we are well on the way to setting him free from the slavery of sin.

You don't eliminate tension by punishing a man. You don't eliminate it by telling him that what he is doing doesn't matter. Every man has a conscience and, while he has a conscience, he must face tension when he sins. You can't eliminate tension by taking medicine or alcohol. No, there is only one way and it has been well-tested for 1900 years. It is still the Gospel of Jesus Christ. It has been expressed in a hundred different ways to meet the needs of many different situations. Can we express it afresh in terms of our modern knowledge of human nature so that instead of losing its power, its power may be all the more available to all who have such desperate need of it?

Well, this is the way I have seen it operate in hundreds of lives in many difficult situations. A soul is at war with itself because of this inner compulsion to sin, this slavery to evil. Again and again an attempt has been made to screw up the will-power to beat the temptation, but the very screwing up of the will-power increases the tension which is such a big part of the problem.

Now if a man can be led to believe in Christ and not only to believe, but to trust Him to the point of handing over the burden of his problem to Him, then the tension is lifted immediately. A man comes to think he is hopeless, thinks he has committed the unpardonable sin. With such an attitude is it any wonder he gives up the struggle? But help him to see that God loves him with an everlasting love, that God will pardon his sin if he whole-heartedly repents of it, then at once he is set free from the burden of the past. The moment we pray with faith, "God take charge of my imagination and my will," the tension is lifted and the power of the temptation greatly reduced. A man is set free from the fear of the future when he comes to see the living Christ as His partner who is able and willing to share His resources with him in the battle ahead. He knows that millions of others have conquered through faith in Christ and when he believes that he too can conquer in the same way, then the burden of fear for the future is lifted. Christ breaks the power of sin in our lives by removing the tension which gives it power.

We are often beaten by our own negative thinking. We can win when we believe that we shall win; in other words, when our minds are filled with positive thoughts. Without faith in Christ, we must be filled with negative thinking and because the mind always tends to develop the picture which we hold in it, if we picture ourselves being defeated, we shall be defeated. On the other hand, faith in Christ enables us to believe and to see ourselves prevailing over the power of sin and that in itself is more than half the battle. As a man thinketh so is he.

(*b*) *Liberty to do what we like.* Not only does Christ give us freedom from the compulsion of sin, He gives us liberty to do what we like. That, of course, needs some explanation. It is not the liberty to do any crazy thing that comes into our heads. When Ruskin was a baby in his nurse's arms, he was fascinated by the brightly polished copper kettle boiling on the hearth. He reached out his finger to touch it and cried when the nurse refused to let him. Then his mother commanded the nurse to let him touch it. Never again did Ruskin seek liberty with a boiling kettle.

We have to learn what is good for us and what is not. You can find out the hard way—or the easy way, by following Jesus Christ. Jesus Christ is the Way, the Truth and the Life and if we follow Him we find that way of life which is wholly satisfying, the way of life ordained of God, the way which leads to the glorious liberty of the children of God. Having come to love him, we know that His will and His laws are best and we rejoice to keep them. In keeping them, we find an ever-increasing expansion of personality, satisfaction and freedom.

It was Augustine who gave us that great motto, "Love God and do what you like." You see what he meant. If you love God, you won't want to do anything that isn't good for you or for others. You will instinctively love the right, rejoice to do it and so feel free, right and happy. Augustine knew what he was talking about. As a young man he was the spoilt only son of a widow and became completely wayward. He broke his mother's heart with his drunkenness and revelry with all sorts of wrong companions. Still, she kept praying for him with faith until the day when Augustine was set free from the slavery of sin by the One who said, "If the Son shall make you free, ye shall be free indeed." Then he became Saint Augustine, one of the greatest intellects ever produced in the long history of the Catholic Church and the one who, perhaps more than any other, preserved the Church through the dark ages which followed the collapse of the Roman Empire.

"Love God and do what you like." I think that among the happiest people I know are the deaconesses of our church who often have far too much to do in some of the worst slums in the country. In spite of all their frustrations, all their disappointments, all their straight-out hardship and self-sacrifice, they are happy and free as few others ever are. They love God and do what they like—which is God's work among those who are most needy.

We all have work to do which sometimes oppresses us. We feel enslaved to it. Jesus Christ can set us free, not by taking us out of that work, but by giving us an entirely new attitude to it. There are scores of girls in our Wednesday congregation who work in government offices. I think of one who had to attend a busy counter visited by hundreds of people every day. Sometimes in government departments the customers develop a negative attitude! They resent regulations and they come looking for a fight. This girl frequently finished the day with a splitting headache. She hated her work and wanted to give it away. Then, lying in bed one Sunday morning, she was twiddling the knob of her radio when she struck a church service and a sermon on the idea that every one of us can serve God through our daily work, that we can take Jesus Christ into partnership and, if we do, the tension that makes our work such a strain can be lifted.

The thought completely changed the girl. She kept repeating to herself, "I can do all things through Christ." She had been yearning to get away and do what she liked. Now, by getting right with God, she found that she could like what she had to do. Because hers was a difficult job with difficult people, it was a bigger opportunity to serve God by serving these difficult people, helping them to a better attitude and making things happier for her whole department. She began to rejoice in her work. She had discovered the liberty of the children of God. Yes, "if the Son shall make you free, ye shall be free indeed."

TONIC CARD

IF THE SON SHALL MAKE YOU FREE, YE SHALL BE FREE INDEED.

> *John* viii. 36.

Love God, and do what you like.

> Augustine.

CHAPTER NINE

CHRIST-LIKE PEACEMAKING

IN DISCUSSING the secret of happiness at the beginning of the Sermon on the Mount, Jesus laid great emphasis on the activity of peacemaking. Indeed he regarded it as being God-like. He said, "Blessed are the peacemakers for they shall be called the children of God." The expression means that peacemakers share the very nature of God.

They also share the happiness of God. What a happy woman Mrs. D'Oyly Carte must have been when she brought together those two temperamental geniuses, Gilbert and Sullivan. They had quarrelled and parted, apparently for ever, but she reconciled them. In their inmost souls they were glad to come together again and thereafter they produced their greatest works, *The Mikado* (regarded as the most successful of all the Savoy operas), *Ruddigore, The Gondoliers* and *The Yeomen of the Guard.* These delightful light operas might have been lost to the world entirely if it had not been for the peacemaker, Mrs. D'Oyly Carte. That is the kind of reward, the kind of happiness which comes to the true peacemaker.

What happiness would be ours if we could have some share in preventing even a minor war between two nations with all the fear, the misery, the heartache and the sin that goes with every war. You may say, what can I do? You may be able to do much. First, let us consider the question at the personal level and, then, at the international level.

I

The first essential in a peacemaker is to realize the supreme importance of peace to God. It is human nature to enjoy a fight, especially a fight between other people in which we have nothing to lose and, indeed, might have much to gain. When told to intervene, we are tempted to say, "It is none of my business." But it is God's business and therefore the duty and privilege of peacemaking is laid on every Christian.

In August, 1950, a young man named Constantine Kefaloghianni swooped out of the darkness outside a movie on the island of Crete and carried off to a cave in the mountains a beautiful 22-year-old girl named Thassoula Petraghiorghi. For generations there had been bitter rivalry between these two families and, when the romance between these two young people was first disclosed, both families were horrified and declared that the thought of marriage was completely out of the question. Now Constantine had taken matters into his own hands.

Thassoula's father declared that he was raising an armed force and was determined to bring her back at all costs. The island was split into two rival factions. The government declared martial law, but it seemed that civil war was inevitable. It was then that the Church stepped in. Archbishop Spyridon of Athens sent a note to the government urging mediation. After conferences with both sides it was agreed that the chief of police would go himself to the mountain hide-out to interview the young couple. If Thassoula wished to marry Constantine, then a marriage would be arranged. If not, Constantine must agree to let her go. This was done and war was averted. The solution began with the will to peace on the part of the Archbishop of Athens.

The second essential in a peacemaker is wisdom

and plenty of it. Anybody can meddle in other people's affairs, but it takes somebody with infinite tact to play the role of the peacemaker successfully. An uncle of mine was a bank manager in Victoria. At one time he was appointed to the suburb of Collingwood and had to live above the bank in the middle of what was then Melbourne's underworld. Out for a walk one evening he was passing the side fence of a shabby home when he heard screams in the backyard. Climbing up on the fence he saw a man attacking his wife with an axe. When shouts had no effect on the man my uncle climbed over the fence and attempted to protect the woman. As he did so he was attacked not only by the man, but also by the woman, for daring to intervene in a perfectly respectable family row! Verily, the way of a peacemaker is hard.

There is, however, an important lesson to be learned from that incident. Although my uncle received no thanks for his intervention, and indeed was lucky to escape without serious injury—his exit over the fence being considerably faster than his entry in the same manner—the fact that he did intervene brought that quarrel to an end. If somebody cares enough to intervene in a quarrel their influence can be considerable even though their action may appear to be resented by both sides.

For this reason and many others the peacemaker must be endowed with inexhaustible patience. He will get little thanks and he will often be abused. He will be so discouraged that he will wonder if it is worth it, but he must be prepared for these things. He will be able to take it only if he constantly remembers that to be a peacemaker is to be a son of God, to share in the quality and nature of God Himself.

The Rev. J. D. Jones, one of the greatest statesmen the Congregational Union of England and Wales had produced was minister of the Richmond Hill church in Bournemouth, England, for thirty-nine years. It is a church seating 1,100 people and it is said that J. D. Jones kept it crowded morning and evening for that incredible time. He had many great qualities, but perhaps his greatest quality of all was that of peacemaking. In Church meetings, J. D. Jones often met with ticklish situations, heat would be generated and, with anyone else in the chair, a real split in the congregation would have developed. J. D. Jones, without sacrificing justice, or righteousness, or truth or any other great principle, made the peace of the church such an ideal for himself and all his congregation, that he succeeded in preserving it for all those years to the immense blessing, not only of the Richmond Hill church, but of the whole Union and indeed of the whole of Christendom. As the Bible constantly reminds us there is no spiritual power in any church which is sundered by petty strife.

The fourth quality I regard as essential in a Christian peacemaker is the readiness to sacrifice self in the cause of peace. We have no higher example of that than the sacrifice of Jesus Himself upon the Cross. Apparently there was no other way whereby peace could be restored between rebellious mankind and God, between man and man and between a man and himself. If we are to continue the divine work of peacemaking in the world, we must be prepared for self-sacrifice.

Consider the truth of that in the story of one of the greatest peacemakers alive today. I refer to Ralph Bunche, who found a solution to the thorny problem of Palestine. Ralph Bunche was born on August 7th, 1904. His father was a barber in Detroit. Both his parents died when Ralph was thirteen. He was then brought up by his grandmother, a tiny woman with a strong character. She taught this Negro boy to be proud of his race, never to accept a slight from anyone, but to bear no bitterness. As newsboy and delivery boy he worked his way through college and won a fellowship at Harvard University where he studied political science and was the first Negro to receive a Ph.D. in that subject. He became a teacher of political science at Howard, the leading American Negro university. In that capacity he was called upon to serve with the United Nations and wrote much of the trusteeship matter in the U.N. Charter. In 1947, the war between the Jews and the Arabs was flaring up again in Palestine and Trygve Lie asked Ralph Bunche to go with the U.N. mediator, Count Folke Bernadotte. Then, in September, 1948, the great peacemaker who had played a vital part in bringing the second World War to a conclusion, was assassinated.

Bunche was now invited to take Bernadotte's place. He knew it might well mean his own assassination, but he accepted. He was not only ready for the supreme sacrifice, he was ready to sacrifice all comfort and even health. He arrived on the island of Rhodes in January, 1949, and he told the deputations meeting there: "I'll never adjourn this meeting. I'll stay here ten years if necessary." Day after day, he presided at what seemed to be hopeless negotiations. Whenever the tension got too great, he would knock off for a game of ping-pong or billiards. At one stage, when a new set of delegates had arrived to discuss one aspect of the general problem, it took Ralph Bunche five days to get them to shake hands before they could start. But he remained serene and patient, not once losing his temper. On another occasion, when he had to reconcile Egypt and Israel, he sat in his room from 10 A.M. right through that day and the next night until six the following morning when they were finally ready to agree. Such was his determination to build peace in the most difficult area on earth.

Within eight months of his appointment, Ralph Bunche, the American Negro, had succeeded. Today the world showers honors upon him, blessing him as a peacemaker and as a son of God.

II

I want to conclude by referring to what the church has done and can do to assist in the promotion of peace at the international level. So many people feel overwhelmed by the immensity of the problem and develop the attitude that anything they can do as individuals would be so infinitesimal it could have no effect on the real problem. Consequently, they do nothing. When millions adopt that attitude nothing is done to prevent war, but history has shown again and again that a comparatively few peacemakers often achieve wonders, particularly if assisted by a friendly public opinion to which we can all contribute.

The World Council of Churches to which most

Protestant churches belong is exercising an increasingly powerful influence for good in world affairs. In 1946 the World Council set up what is known as the C.C.I.A.—the Churches' Commision on International Affairs. This commission originally consisted of representatives from about twenty-four countries and was headed by an outstanding triumvirate in the persons of a Dutchman, an Englishman and an American. The commission and these three leaders in particular have been in close touch with the great national leaders who control international affairs. For instance, in the Korean conflict, Dr. Frederick Nolde, the American leader of the commission, travelled to Korea with General Eisenhower. Because of his influence and the influence of other Christian leaders, three tragedies in Korea were averted; the area of fighting was not enlarged as some wanted it enlarged, atomic weapons were not used and negotiations for peace were commenced when they were and were not indefinitely delayed. A proposal of Dr. Nolde's in regard to the treatment of prisoners (involving the principles of non-forceable detention and non-forceable repatriation), solved one of the most difficult problems holding up negotiations. The principle he laid down that we stood for unity in Korea, but not by military force, was also accepted.

In another direction, the C.C.I.A. proposed (in

August, 1950) a system of International Peace Observer Commissions to be sent to any danger spots. By keeping an eye on any deteriorating situation, they can report back to the United Nations while there is still time to make peace and before war has actually begun. One such commission was operating in the Balkans in 1953.

Then again the World Council of Churches and the C.C.I.A., representing 161 different churches in 48 different countries, have made the great nations realize that peace must be built on justice, truth, kindness and brotherhood. Accordingly, wherever there is starvation, sickness, ignorance or fear upon the face of the earth, there is a danger to peace.

In 1953, the United Nations Appeal for children raised nearly $14,000,000 bringing relief to 70,-000,000 diseased and hungry children. The World Health Organization is fighting malaria, T.B., yaws and other diseases on a global scale. UNESCO is doing much to rectify world ignorance, facing the fact that half the world's population still cannot read or write. The United Nations Program of Technical Assistance together with the Food and Agriculture Organization is working on the problem of the world's food; three-quarters of the population of the globe still live in appalling poverty. For the first time in history, the United Nations assembled an international army to fight aggression. The United Nations has assisted in stopping three wars— in Palestine, Indonesia and Kashmir—each one of which might have been a spark to set the world aflame. This is something of what the United Nations has done and do you know what it costs you? It costs each American less than the price of a pack of cigarettes per year.

I have lumped together the World Council of Churches and the United Nations in my discussion of peacemaking at the international level. I think it is right to do so. To a very great degree, Christian principles have been applied to the international problem through the U.N. The Declaration of Human Rights would have been impossible without Christianity. We may not agree with every decision made in the United Nations, but seen in its entirety and while it is guided by the Christian conscience of the World Church, it is far and away the greatest hope we have for peace among the nations.

The World Council of Churches has its own department for relieving distress, particularly among refugees who are in need not only of physical comfort but also of spiritual comfort. In 1952, the churches of the world raised nearly $12,000,000 for this great work, which in itself is a magnificent contribution to world peace. You can be a peacemaker, even at the international level, by working for and through your own church right where you are. "Blessed are the peacemakers for they shall be called the children of God."

TONIC CARD

**BLESSED ARE THE PEACEMAKERS
FOR THEY SHALL BE CALLED THE CHILDREN
OF GOD.**

Matthew v. 9.

We can do no more Christ-like service than continually to promote peace, to keep people from drifting apart, and to draw friends and neighbors closer together in love.

J. R. Miller

CHAPTER TEN

PURITY OF SOUL

W E COME NOW to consider the greatest happiness of all and how we may enter into it.
Throughout the Bible and especially in the New
Testament there is a constant emphasis on the truth
that the greatest experience that can come to any
man is the experience of knowing God. "This is life
eternal," said Jesus, "to know Thee and Him whom
Thou hast sent." In the Beatitude which forms the
text for this chapter we are assured, "Blessed are the
pure in heart, for they shall see God." This presents
us with a difficulty at the start because as we are told
in the first chapter of John, "No man hath seen God
at any time." It is manifestly impossible to "see" an

infinite God with the physical eye. What then did Jesus mean when He said, "Blessed are the pure in heart for they shall see God?" We shall consider first what is meant by seeing God and then how we may achieve this great experience.

I

No man has "seen" God at any time with the physical eye, but plenty of people have experienced God. I have permission to share with you two experiences which came to members of St. Stephen's. One of them wrote as follows:

"I had a wonderful experience of hearing the morning stars singing together once, and only once. It came after a night of sadness and tears, after a simple prayer that I be given the power to rise above my unhappiness. I fell into a deep sleep which lasted unbroken for the rest of the night. I awakened suddenly and completely—all trace of sleep had left me. It was that quiet mystic hour preceding the full dawn, and I wondered for the moment where such wonderful music could be coming from at such an hour.

"Wide awake, yet keeping very still, almost holding my breath so that I might not miss a note of the most wonderful music I had ever heard, I lay there listening, spell-bound. Listening intently to it, I knew it was not the music of one person's

making, but it seemed to be a vast orchestra playing an accompaniment to a full choir of voices in
the background.

"I turned my head, raising it a little, trying to
distinguish the direction from which it was coming. All I saw were the lovely early morning stars
shining in the deep blue of the sky. Then the mystery proving too much for me, I arose and walked
out on the small verandah adjoining. There were
no lights to be seen anywhere or in any of the
neighboring houses. I returned to my bed. The
silence was so profound, and one might say, so
deep, that I could almost feel it. I then realized
that the music I was hearing came out of that
great silence, out from that star-filled morning
sky. I was listening to the morning stars singing
together.

"The melody was indescribably beautiful. I had
heard nothing like it before or since, yet, as I men-
tioned, the silence was unbroken by any earthly
sound. I lay there knowing I had been granted a
lovely and unusual spiritual experience—that in
spite of sorrow comes beauty and harmony if we
will try and make it so. Fighting against the sleep
that threatened to overpower me again, I listened
to the Song of Creation, for that is the song of the
morning stars, the great eternal song they are always singing, could we but hear it. Some day we
shall all be so in tune and in harmony that we
shall readily hear the great music of the Universe.

"I managed to keep awake, but the music gradually became fainter and far away. I listened, hop-

ing it would come back again, and after some
time I noticed I was hearing with my physical ear
the everyday sounds—the morning songs, and
squabbling too, of the birds and here and there
the unromantic, but necessary, sound of the milk
carts."

That experience given to me by an educated and
intelligent member of my church reminded me of a
film we saw recently in the church hall. It was a
color film depicting the use of a new device called
a hydrophone which is a microphone for use under
water. People had always assumed there was no
sound in the ocean and referred to it as the "silent
deep," but it is not silent at all for those who have
ears to hear. So no doubt there are heavenly sounds
and great spiritual experiences waiting for those
capable of hearing such sounds and entering into
such experiences.

Another member of St. Stephen's is a highly
qualified nurse who was taken seriously ill. For a
time she must have been very close to death. While
recovering she saw a vision of the Cross. It was a
shining Cross appearing above and in front of the
doorway of her room. She assured me that she felt
greatly lifted up and helped by this experience. What
interested me was that, as she told me about it, her
own face became quite radiant. We could multiply
such experiences endlessly and all of them, I believe,

are an experience of God. All come under the heading of "seeing God" in the spiritual sense.

It is an interesting thing that man is so made that consciously or unconsciously he strives after the experience of God. A man may tell himself that he doesn't need God and may pretend that he is getting along all right without Him, but it is bluff. Man is so made that right round the world today in one form or another he is seeking God, just as down through the centuries his forebears have always sought Him knowing that there is no final happiness and no real contentment until God is found.

Because that is true, men of faith have never been afraid of death. Indeed, when the time has come, they have welcomed it as an opportunity to see God. The great Lord Tennyson summed it up in the hymn:

Sunset and evening star,
And one clear call to me!
And may there be no moaning of the bar,
When I put out to sea.

Twilight and evening bell,
And after that the dark!
And may there be no sadness of farewell
When I embark;

For, though from out our bourne of Time
and Place

The flood may bear me far,
I hope to see my Pilot face to face
When I have crossed the bar.

II

Deep down in all of us is this yearning to "see our pilot face to face." In all of us there is a recognition that purity is essential for such an experience. Now purity in the spiritual sense involves two things.

(*a*) *Cleanness.* From the beginning of time followers of the great religions have recognized the need to come before God with clean hands and a clean heart. Remember the words of the 24th Psalm:

"Who shall ascend into the hill of the Lord?
Or who shall stand in His holy place?
He that hath clean hands and a pure heart;
Who hath not lifted up his soul unto vanity,
nor sworn deceitfully."

Any of us can test this law for ourselves. If our hearts are full of uncleanness—of malice, or hatred, or pride or selfishness or anything else that is unclean in God's sight then we can't get through to God. A fine young man wrote to me the other day from another state asking me why his prayers no longer have any reality. He says that he prays every night going to bed, but his prayers don't seem to be getting

through. God does not seem real. Now I know that
in his case there is much in his life that is wrong.
I don't mean that he has done anything illegal or
committed any great sin. His friends would all assure
you that he is a very respectable young man and they
think highly of him. But as have a good many other
young people in the late teens and early twenties, he
has developed a state of tension with his parents. On
the one hand, they can't appreciate the fact that he
is now grown up and wants to run his own life. As
he puts it, they are "on his back." It has been going
on for years.

For a long time he was obedient and did what they
wished even when he greatly resented it. He suppressed the resentment into his unconscious mind
where it produced conflict and built up tension.
Today the suppressed rage of the last few years is
making him hit back at his parents and he knows
that is wrong, even though he believes it is their
fault. All this has produced a state of mind which is
"impure." So he cannot find God. That family situation has to be sorted out and this young man has
to get clean inside himself before he will rediscover
reality in his prayers. When he is pure in heart again,
he will "see God."

The religious Jews in the days of Jesus laid great
stress on ceremonial purity. They went to great
trouble to wash themselves and the utensils they

used in worship, just as the Mohammedans do today. There is a well or fountain at every mosque so that worshippers can be clean when they worship. Jesus turned on such people and said, "You are a lot of hypocrites. What is the use of washing the outside of a cup if the inside, which really matters, is still dirty? You are like a lot of white-washed graves— outwardly clean enough, but inwardly full of putre- faction. You will not find God." No, it is the clean heart, the pure heart that is needed.

(*b*) *Singleness of Heart*. At the same time there is another meaning to purity that we must emphasize. After all, cleanness might be the same as emptiness. The purity that Jesus seeks is purity of purpose, singleness of heart. When we talk about pure gold, we mean not just clean gold, but solid gold, no alloy, no dross. If with all your heart ye truly seek Him, ye shall find Him. The Greek word for pure here is "katharos" and in the old days there was an expres- sion "to katharon tou stratou," meaning the clean part of the army, or the portion of the army that was unfettered and fit for active service. It is the portion of the army which won the victories. So it is that the whole-hearted believer, free from all worldly bonds or fetters, is the one who enters into the Di- vine Presence and "sees God."

No one is quite so free from worldly fetters or impurities, worldly desires or interests, as a child at

Christmas time. Christmas is intensely real to a child
and it is the happiest time of his life because he is
pure in the sense of being spiritually clean and because he has such singleness of heart. No wonder
Jesus said, "Except ye turn and become as a little
child ye cannot enter the Kingdom of God." It was
to the child Samuel that the great experience of God
came, not to Eli who was soiled by the cares and the
sordidness of the world and his own family. "Blessed
are the pure in heart for they shall see God."

III

The question then is, "How do we become pure?"
Do we do it by our own effort or is it the gift of God?
Personally I think both are required. That nurse
to whom I referred earlier has a reputation for re-
maining calm and efficient in the operating room
no matter how much panic is raging. She tells me
that, when she is tempted to let go as the others do,
she tries to picture the face of Jesus Christ, tries to
think of Him as being there in the midst. That
steadies her and keeps her pure. There is nothing
like living with the Christ to keep you pure.

One who knew the love of God in Christ and
because of it retained the spirit of a trusting child
all his life was Dean Stanley, perhaps the most outstanding figure of the Church of England a century

ago. In his later years, he was appointed Dean of Westminster Abbey. Crowds thronged to hear him preach, especially in a series of Saturday afternoon addresses on the Beatitudes. But his health was failing and the last Beatitude he took was this one, "Blessed are the pure in heart, for they shall see God." He illustrated the truth of it by pointing round the Abbey to the monuments of great men and women whose lives bore testimony to it. But his hearers all felt that his own life was the best testimony of all. He was essentially a believer who was pure of heart. A little more than a week later he had entered into the eternal presence to see God face to face. Yes, blessed are the pure in heart for they shall see God.

TONIC CARD

BLESSED ARE THE PURE IN HEART: FOR THEY SHALL SEE GOD.

Matthew v. 8.

Help me to keep my heart clean and to live so honestly and fearlessly that no outward failure can dishearten me, or take away the joy of conscious integrity.

CHAPTER ELEVEN

STRAIGHT LIVING

D R. ERNEST WHITE of London's Harley Street, where all the famous specialists are, records the case of a man of thirty-five who came to him complaining of an intense fear of becoming insane. For months he had been suffering from insomnia, loss of appetite and abdominal pain. His main problem was a feeling of panic and nameless dread. At one stage he decided he had appendicitis. He lost still more weight and finally had to give up his work.

Dr. White treated him and managed to restore him sufficiently to enable him to return to work. He was, however, still far from well and he kept returning to the doctor for further treatment. Fi-

135

nally, Dr. White decided that there was only one thing for it and one day he said to the young man. "What you need to do to get well is to return to the God of your youth. For years you have turned your back on God. If you repent and seek forgiveness, you will be restored to full health." The patient was very angry, said he had not consulted a psychologist to be told that, flung down his fee and walked out. After two weeks he telephoned in great distress and asked Dr. White if he would see him again. Dr. White agreed to do so in his own home that night and, after a long talk, the young man knelt down and asked forgiveness from God. The Harley Street specialist records this about him: "Within a month the alteration in him was striking. He completely lost his symptoms, put on weight and was happy and well. Two years later, on leaving for another part of the country, he telephoned me to say how fit he felt and that the last two years had been the happiest and healthiest of his life."

Doctors, and especially those who treat people suffering from nerves, are realizing more and more that, just as you must keep the laws of health if you want a healthy body, so there are certain laws of the spirit you must keep if you want a healthy mind, peace and inward happiness. Jesus said, "Blessed are they that hunger and thirst after righteousness, for they shall be filled." St. Paul wrote, "The Kingdom of God is righteousness and peace and joy." The Psalmist's first words in the first psalm were "Blessed is the man that walketh not in the counsel of the ungodly."

There has grown up a tragic attitude in far too many people today that it is all right to ignore the moral law as long as you can get away with it. Their attitude seems to be, "Lie and steal and take bribes and give them—everybody does it. Why worry?"

You may bluff other people but you can't bluff God and you can't bluff your own conscience. Sooner or later these things will catch up with you, undermine your health and your happiness. At regular intervals we see suicides produced by tortured nerves. Why have the nerves been tortured? Usually because of a deviation from righteousness.

One of the most powerful parts of that magnificent film, *The Robe,* was the portrayal of Marcellus, the Roman tribune, as he returned on the galley-ship to Rome after his term of service in Palestine. During that sojourn, it had fallen to his lot to preside at the crucifixion of Jesus Christ. He had been brought up in a rugged Roman school and the sight of blood was no novelty to him, but there was something about this Man that was different. The crucifixion troubled his conscience. On the ship he tried to sleep. Above him the slaves were toiling at the oars. To mark the time for the oarsmen a man was striking a kind of anvil with a hammer. Every blow went right through Marcellus. Half awake he saw the nails being driven into the hands of Christ. At last, distracted, he rushed on deck screaming to them to stop. They decided he was out of his mind. It was enough to drive any man insane. In the same film, Pilate calls for water to wash his hands although he has just done so. Preoccupied with his own guilt, he has acquired this compulsion. Tradition has it that to the end of his days Pilate was everlastingly washing his hands in a vain attempt to remove the guilt from his own soul.

Guilt and happiness can never go together. God has given us a right way to live. Follow his laws and life becomes a rich and noble thing. Defy those laws and, although we may appear to get away with it for a time and even prosper in a material sense, sooner or later we must pay the price with the loss of our inner peace and happiness in this world, whatever may follow for us in the next.

How different it is with those who have a clear conscience, who know the joy of conscious integrity! When Charles Spurgeon was at the height of his power as a preacher, drawing 6,000 people twice a Sunday to London's Metropolitan Tabernacle, a man thought to trade upon his huge reputation by frightening him into paying over money. He wrote him a letter saying that if he did not receive a specified sum within two days he would publish certain things which would quickly put an end to Spurgeon's influence and popular esteem. Spurgeon replied in these words, "You and your like are requested to publish all you know about me across the heavens." A man who can say that sort of thing is strong, serene and happy.

* * *

We have, I hope, established the point that to be happy we must obey the laws of God, which means also the divinely inspired laws of society. "Do the right and fear no man" is a great maxim. There is no greater enemy of happiness than fear. But as soon as we talk about happiness depending on keeping the law we are reminded that the New Testament is full of warnings of the dangers of this kind of life:

(1) People who are strict about obeying the laws of God and man too often become self-righteous prigs or hypocrites or both. Nobody detested such people more heartily than Jesus Christ.

(2) The law tends to become such a tyrant that we become obsessed with dread at the thought of breaking one jot or tittle of it and happiness evaporates.

(3) Although we have the Ten Commandments

and other plain teaching as to what is the law of God, life is far from simple and the applications of various laws become so complicated that we are confused and we don't know what to do. The law is like a schoolmaster, said Paul, and while we are at school the master tells us what to do and we know where we are. The trouble comes when we leave school and the master is not there to tell us what to do. Uncertainty and confusion are likewise the enemy of happiness.

(4) Perhaps the greatest disadvantage of the law, as Paul also reminds us, is that it actually suggests sins to us which would not occur to us if we were not so obsessed with keeping the law.

Here then is our dilemma. We can't be happy unless our lives are righteous. We need the law to make our lives righteous, yet the law itself is a danger to our happiness. Let us turn back to the teachings of Jesus to see what answer He gives.

At first sight, He seems to make things worse than ever. He tightens up the law. In the Sermon on the Mount, He said, "Ye have heard that it was said by them of old time, Thou shalt not kill; and whosoever shall kill shall be in danger of the judgment: but I say unto you that whosoever is angry with his brother without a cause shall be in danger of the judgment." Again Jesus said, "Ye have heard that it was said by them of old time, Thou shalt not commit adultery: but I say unto you that whosoever looketh on a woman to lust after her hath committed adultery with her already in his heart."

It would seem that we are all murderers and adulterers, but let us consider just what Jesus really meant. For one thing notice that the anger He condemns is blind and continuing anger without a cause. He himself was angry when there was cause for it. Again, in regard to adultery, we cannot help impure thoughts coming to us. It is when a man looks at a woman to lust after her (that is with the intention of committing adultery with her) that he has, says Jesus, already committed that sin though no action has taken place. It is the purpose, the motive, the intention, that is important.

Now that brings me to our Lord's attitude to the law. The key word is "inwardness." The Pharisees of His day treated the law as an outward thing. As long as they kept it in outward appearances, it did not worry them what was happening to their spirits. Jesus said the law must be written in your heart. The spirit of the law of God must be in your spirit and through and through. That being so, we might appear sometimes to break the outward law, but if the spirit is right, all is well.

We have an example of that when Jesus and

His disciples were walking through the cornfield on the Sabbath day. According to the pettifogging law of those days, if you picked one ear of wheat that was reaping and if you ground the corn in your hand that was milling. Well, our Lord and His disciples were hungry. They picked some ears of wheat, ground them up in their hands and ate them on the Sabbath day. The Pharisees were horrified. The men were breaking the strict law of the Sabbath. Jesus said, "What was the purpose of the law? To help men, not to hinder them or hurt them. The Sabbath was made for man, not man for the Sabbath." Jesus and His disciples had done nothing to destroy the real value of the Sabbath. The law did not expect them to fast every Sabbath. They had to eat. No, it is not the outward keeping of the law that makes for happiness. It is the inward spirit that is important.

How can you be sure that your inward spirit is in harmony with the will of God? Jesus gave us the answer quite simply. Love God and love your fellows and you can't go wrong. As Paul puts it (Gal. v. 14), "For all the law is fulfilled in one word, even in this; Thou shalt love thy neighbor as thyself." How can we love God? By loving our neighbor and above all by loving Jesus Christ. The more we study His life, the more we seek His presence, the more we love Him, His spirit enters into us so that we automatically keep the law of God even though we may never have read the Ten Commandments.

*   *   *

It is the great positive side of the truth that I would leave with you in the words of Jesus (Matthew v. 6), "Blessed are they which do hunger and thirst after righteousness for they shall be filled." It is not just that by keeping the law we are happy because we avoid punishment. That is a negative kind of happiness that doesn't satisfy anybody. No, Jesus meant that if we hunger and thirst after the spirit of righteousness, which is the spirit of God Himself and His own spirit, then we shall have that spirit and we shall be wholly satisfied. Some translators prefer the word "goodness" to "righteousness" in this text and that will further emphasize the kind of spirit that is meant.

The Greek word for "filled" is the word used when we take a poor, starved, drought-stricken animal, at the point of death for lack of food, and not merely give it enough food to avert death, but to restore it to normality and eventually fatten it until it is a really fine animal in every respect. If we hunger and thirst after the spirit of goodness that was in Jesus, then we shall be given that spirit and we shall find our souls satisfied.

Several years ago there was a young man who took

to drink while serving in the navy. During the war, he married the daughter of a minister and in due course three children arrived. It should have been a happy home, but it was not because of the husband's compulsion to drink. There were times when he became really violent. He began to steal and lie to get more drink. Unrighteousness was bringing misery into that home. They tried to reason with him, but it was no use. He said he liked his alcohol and he wasn't going to give it up for anybody.

It so happened that one day I was asked to give an address on the work of Alcoholics Anonymous to a group of people in which the man's father-in-law was present. During question time this minister stood up, told his story and said that things were now so bad that they were planning to take his daughter and the three children away, it being no longer safe for them to stay in the home. Was there anything A.A. could do in that case? I said "No, A.A. could not do anything until the alcoholic himself expressed a willingness to accept help. But," I went on, "there is the power of prayer and I suggest that all here pray now for a change of heart in that young man."

We did and a week later the minister came to see me again. Once more there were tears in his eyes, but this time they were tears of joy. He said, "He came to me last night and he used the very phrase which you used last week. He said he had a change of heart. I am sure there is a new spirit in him." There was a new spirit, a new spirit of righteousness, a new spirit of goodness and a great new day had dawned for the whole family, a day of happiness.

Blessed are they which do hunger and thirst after righteousness for they shall be filled.

TONIC CARD

BLESSED ARE THEY WHICH DO HUNGER AND THIRST AFTER RIGHTEOUSNESS: FOR THEY SHALL BE FILLED.

Matthew v. 6.

To get to Heaven; turn right and keep straight.

CHAPTER TWELVE

GLAD GENEROSITY

HAPPINESS and giving always go together. It is a happy thing to receive. Jesus surprised men by teaching them that it is a happier thing to give. Properly understood this is, of course, perfectly true. Let us then try to understand just what Jesus meant:

To begin with, let us recognize the truth that if you only give in order to be happy you will be more miserable than ever. If you only give in order to receive you must face the disillusionment and final despair of all who live selfish lives. On the other hand, if your giving is the expression of the genuine love that is within you then others benefit and you

can't help receiving benefit. That is the main point
I want to make. You can't give without receiving.

I

The late Louis B. Mayer, founder of Metro-Gold-
wyn-Mayer, once told about an experience in his
childhood. He had a fight with another boy and lost.
While his mother was bathing his black eye he told
her how it was entirely the fault of the other boy that
the fight had started. His mother said nothing, but
when the bathing was completed, she took Louis
to the back door of their home. Nearby were several
hills which created a fine echo. She told him to call
those hills all the bad names he could think of. He
did so and the bad names all came back to him.
"Now," she said, "call out, 'God bless you'." He did
so and back came "God bless you." Louis B. Mayer
said he never forgot that lesson. What you give to
others you get back from them. He built his life
on that principle and made quite a success of it.

I remember the same principle operating once in
an airplane. We were flying from Adelaide to Melbourne. The plane was full of individual business
men. To judge from appearances, they seemed to
have no connection with one another, nor did they
appear to desire any connection. In due course,
the hostess appeared out of the cockpit section and

handed the flight card to the passenger in the front
seat. He read it and turning to the man beside him
handed him the card, giving him a friendly smile
as he did so. I noticed that this man returned the
smile and as he leaned over the seat to hand it to
the one behind him gave another smile. That smile
was given and received and given again right down
the airliner until it reached one sour individual who
did not smile. So the delightful chain was broken.
From that point onwards the glum looks continued.
We are all individuals, we are all free and we can
all break the chain, but generally speaking what we
give we receive.

On that same aircraft were two men returning to
their homes after spending several weeks in Adelaide
on business. They had both stayed at good hotels
and as far as the lines they represented were concerned, they should have had a prosperous visit. I
asked each man independently how he found the
Adelaide people. The first man said he found them
cold, unfriendly and uncooperative. I had lived in
Adelaide for three and a half years and I felt disappointed and hurt by this description of a people
whom I regarded as my own. Later, on the same
flight, I talked to the second man and asked him
the same question. His reply was the direct opposite.
He found the Adelaide people warm, hospitable,
friendly and cooperative almost to an embarrassing

degree. How could two people get such divergent impressions of the same people? The truth was that the first man himself was cold, unfriendly and uncooperative and with what measure he had "meted" it had been "meted" to him again. The second man was warm, friendly and cooperative so he had been met with warmth, friendship and cooperation. We should be very careful in describing other people. Nearly always we describe ourselves. Give and it shall be given unto you—exactly what you give.

It is true that you receive the same kind of thing as you give. But Jesus went on to say "good measure, pressed down and shaken together and running over." In other words, you will always get more than what you give. If you give evil, you will get still more evil. If you sow what is good, you will reap a still greater harvest of good. It applies in business and it applies in church affairs. Some years ago a director of a world-famous soap firm decided that the company was spending too much on advertising. He argued with the other members of his board that the firm was well-established and well-known. They could afford to run on their reputation. All this advertising was beneath their dignity, he thought. Besides it was costing too much money. Eventually he persuaded them to cut their advertising budget by 5 per cent. It was not as much as he wanted, but it did save several thousand pounds. Or did it? When they checked, they found their sales had dropped 5 per cent and they had lost many thousands of pounds. You must spend in order to profit. You must give in order to receive.

The same principle has operated with our Wednesday services and Tonic cards. These services have been entirely maintained by people who gladly give of their time and energy and money. Nobody is paid a penny. I received no extra stipend when they were introduced and I don't want any. The organist is a volunteer. Every member of the choir is a volunteer. Other volunteers put the orders of service in the hymn-books, and others again give out the books and later receive the offering and count it. It takes another volunteer a whole evening to check the offering and prepare it for the bank. In twelve months, these offerings contributed over $3,600 to help pay for 180,000 tonic prayer cards. In that sense those cards have been a gift to the community from this congregation. In the same period the Wednesday congregation has also given away another $5,400 to good causes of one kind and another. If Jesus was right when He said, "Give and it shall be given unto you," we ought to be seeing some results. Well, are we not? The size and strength of my congregation—over a thousand strong week after week—is surely proof that you don't grow weaker by giving. The spiritual strength of the congregation and the healing power which has gone out to scores for whom this congregation has prayed is further proof of the same principle. When we began praying for individuals, I admit I wondered if it was wise. Now, beyond any shadow of doubt, I know that tremendous power for the healing of spirit and mind and body goes out from this great congregation which is founded so much on the spirit of giving.

Let us lift our sights higher still and look at Jesus Christ. He had no money to give, but He was always giving what He had, His wisdom, His healing power, above all His love to those who needed it. He gave Himself. What happened? Men gave themselves to Him and for Him.

II

If you seek to give happiness to others, you can't do it without happiness coming back to yourself together with the strength that goes with happiness.

A few years ago a fifty-two-year-old woman lost her husband. Her life was so dark and she felt so depressed she decided to go and live in the sunshine of Miami in Florida. Day by day she would sit in the park. There was plenty of sunshine round about her, but little in her heart. She was short of money and this together with her grief and loneliness made a dark cloud over her spirit. She had a faith of sorts and she prayed for guidance.

No answer seemed to come until Christmas Day. With so many others enjoying themselves she, in her loneliness, felt worse than ever. Then came the guidance for which she had been waiting. An inner voice seemed to say to her, "Go over to the recreation house in the park." She was so weak by now she could scarcely make the distance and, when she arrived, she saw a number of drab and unhappy-looking pensioners who were hating Christmas just as much as she was. Still the same urge moved her forward and she found herself sitting at a piano. It seemed an obvious thing to play a Christmas carol. Presently over her shoulder she heard the quivering voice of an old man singing. Slowly others joined and soon they were all singing Christmas carols and they had a wonderful time. Week after week she came back and hundreds of these poorer folk would gather to share in the singing.

Today this woman who was so feeble she only wanted to die when she was fifty-two, leads between three thousand and five thousand people singing the old folk songs and the hymns of faith. She has become one of the most dynamic personalities of Mi̇ami. She was beaten and down, depressed and unhappy, until she started to give a little happiness to others and then a great flood of happiness returned to her.

"Give and it shall be given unto you," said Jesus,

"good measure, pressed down and shaken together, and running over." Yes, and if men do that, how much more will God bestow His rich rewards upon those who give.

III

Let us now apply this same principle to the development of personality. If you want to conserve and increase your physical strength, you don't do it by refusing to use your strength or give it. The man who says he wants to be strong and refuses to waste any of his physical energy in exercise soon finds his physical energy fading away. We build up energy by using it, giving it away. If that is true of our muscles, it is still more true of our brains. Brain-power is not increased by refusing to use our brains. We increase their power. So too with the emotional side of our nature. Refuse to show emotion and you lose the capacity to feel emotion. The more you feel, the more you can feel. The more you give of strength or brain or feeling, the more you have to give.

Carry that principle up to the highest activity of man and you see how it affects personality. Nothing is more important to the rich development of personality than love. An intelligent and highly-trained woman who deals with many people in distress every day remarked to me recently, "You know, a woman needs to be loved." That is true, but it is not confined to women. Children desperately need love. Men need love. The aged need love. Without love, the personality withers and dies. If you want love, you must love. Give love and love shall be given unto you. Dr. Robert Oppenheimer, the great genius of the atomic age, has theories about everything. His theory about bringing up his two children is this, "Just pour in the love and it will come out."

There may be some who out of a bitter experience will say to me: "But that isn't true. I loved and love was not given in return." That indeed is tragedy, but let me leave a thought with you and one more true story to drive it home. You can't love God without God's love returning to you. We all need love and the infinite love of God is there waiting for us when we provide the channel. When there is faith and love for Jesus Christ on our part, the channel is created whereby the love of God pours into our souls.

That discovery was the turning point in the life of a young man I met the other day. He lives in Chatswood, a suburb of Sydney, and his name is Bruce McLean. In January, Bruce was stricken with poliomyelitis. For months he could not walk. He lay in the Prince Henry Hospital finding, as many other patients have found, that poliomyelitis can be dreadfully depressing. Bruce McLean tells me that he found Christ was the answer to depression. He says this discovery came through a number of channels: reading, visits from his minister and members of the youth fellowship of his church, radio broadcasts from my church and other religious sessions. In particular, he refers to a visit to the hospital every Sunday night by an evangelistic group. The patients were invited to nominate hymns and every time there would be a chorus shouting for the hymn, "Tell me the old, old story of Jesus and His love." Note the emphasis on love! In a letter to me Bruce has described his discovery in these words:

"Faith, hope and love can be a great blessing in assisting a person to recover from an illness like polio where so much depends on the patient's own efforts and will to recover. Faith and hope are certainly necessary, but greater than these is a full realization of God's amazing love shown at Calvary. Only the Great Physician Himself can bind up the broken-hearted. The Rev. Vernon Turner's 'Sunshine Hour' broadcast was particularly helpful to me. The idea of God's love being like sunshine was a revolutionary concept. I had always tended to regard God's love as an abstract doctrine to be believed by the mind rather than a precious soul-thrilling experience of 'sunshine in my soul.' Probably there are thousands of other people who think of God's love as a doctrine and nothing more."

If that is how it is with you, if you yearn for an assurance of that love of God as something more than an abstract belief, then remember that Jesus has given you the answer. Give and it shall be given unto you. Love God and all the riches and sunshine, the strength and the glory of the love of God will flood your waiting soul.

TONIC CARD

GIVE AND IT SHALL BE GIVEN UNTO YOU.
Luke vi. 38.

The least disciple need not say
"There are no alms to give away"
If love be in the heart.
Rita Snowden.

THE AUTHOR AND HIS BOOK

GORDON POWELL *is minister of St. Stephen's Presbyterian Church in Sydney, Australia. This church probably has the largest attendance of any Protestant church in Australia. More than a thousand persons regularly partake of Holy Communion on Communion Sundays, and the lunch-hour service on Wednesdays, which attracts the largest mid-week congregation in the world, is broadcast by seventeen radio stations, in four states of Australia, to an area covering ninety per cent of the population. Born in 1911 in Warrnambool, Victoria, Mr. Powell is a third generation Australian. He was educated at Melbourne and Glasgow Universities, and during World War II served as a chaplain with the R.A.A.F. in the New Guinea area and on the mainland of Australia. His first church in Australia was at Port Adelaide. After the war he accepted an invitation to be Guest Minister at the Collins Street Independent Church, Melbourne, one of the strongest Congregational churches anywhere, and remained there five and a half years. He is married to the former Gwenyth Ethelwyn Gilchrist, and with their four children they live in Vaucluse, New South Wales. Mr. Powell's first book,* Two Steps to Tokyo, *was published by Oxford University Press, Melbourne, in 1945, and was a best-selling Australian war book. In 1948 Oxford published his second book,* Personal Peace and Power. *Hodder and Stoughton, London, publishers of his more recent books,* The Blessing of Belief, *1956, and* The Secret of Serenity, *1957, also published the British edition of* Happiness is a Habit *in 1954. The book has since had seven printings.*

HAPPINESS IS A HABIT *(Hawthorn, 1960) was designed by Sidney Feinberg and completely manufactured by American Book-Stratford Press, Inc. The body type was set on the Linotype in Baskerville, a modern reproduction of the types cut in 1760 by John Baskerville, of Birmingham, England, reflecting the style of stone inscriptions.*